Multilingual Matters

"Bilingualism: Basic Principles" (Second edition)
HUGO BAETENS BEARDSMORE
"Evaluating Bilingual Education: A Canadian Case Study"
MERRILL SWAIN and SHARON LAPKIN
"Bilingual Children: Guidance for the Family"
GEORGE SAUNDERS
"Language Attitudes Among Arabic-French Bilinguals in Morocco"
ABDELÂLI BENTAHILA
"Conflict and Language Planning in Quebec"
RICHARD Y. BOURHIS (ed.)
"Bilingualism and Special Education"
JIM CUMMINS
"Bilingualism or Not: The Education of Minorities"
TOVE SKUTNABB-KANGAS
"An Ethnographic/Sociolinguistic Approach to Language Proficiency Assessment"
CHARLENE RIVERA (ed.)
"Communicative Competence Approaches to Language Proficiency Assessment:
Research and Application"
CHARLENE RIVERA (ed.)
"Language Proficiency and Academic Achievement"
CHARLENE RIVERA (ed.)
"Pluralism: Cultural Maintenance and Evolution"
BRIAN BULLIVANT
"Placement Procedures in Bilingual Education: Education and Policy Issues"
CHARLENE RIVERA (ed.)
"The Education of Linguistic and Cultural Minorities in the OECD Countries"
STACY CHURCHILL
"Learner Language and Language Learning"
CLAUS FAERCH, KIRSTEN HAASTRUP and ROBERT PHILLIPSON
"Bilingual and Multicultural Education: Canadian Perspectives"
STAN SHAPSON and VINCENT D'OYLEY (eds.)
"Multiculturalism: The Changing Australian Paradigm"
LOIS FOSTER and DAVID STOCKLEY
"Language Acquisition of a Bilingual Child"
ALVINO FANTINI
"Modelling and Assessing Second Language Acquisition"
KENNETH HYLTENSTAM and MANFRED PIENEMANN (eds.)
"Aspects of Bilingualism in Wales"
COLIN BAKER
"Minority Education and Ethnic Survival"
MICHAEL BYRAM
"Age in Second Language Acquisition"
BIRGIT HARLEY
"Language in a Black Community"
VIV EDWARDS
"Language and Education in Multilingual Settings"
BERNARD SPOLSKY (ed.)
"The Interdisciplinary Study of Urban Bilingualism in Brussels"
ELS WITTE and HUGO BAETENS BEARDSMORE (eds.)
"Introspection in Second Language Research"
CLAUS FAERCH and GABRIELE KASPER (eds.)
"Talk and Social Organisation"
GRAHAM BUTTON and JOHN R.E. LEE

Please contact us for the latest book information:
Multilingual Matters, Bank House, 8a Hill Road,
Clevedon, Avon BS21 7HH, England.

Raising Children Bilingually:
The Pre-School Years

MULTILINGUAL MATTERS 27

Raising Children Bilingually: The Pre-School Years

Lenore Arnberg

MULTILINGUAL MATTERS LTD
Clevedon · Philadelphia

Library of Congress Cataloging-in-Publication Data

Arnberg, Lenore, 1947–
  Raising children bilingually.

  Bibliography: p.
  1. Bilingualism in children   2. Child rearing.
  3. Child development.   4. Language acquisition.   I. Title.
  P115.2.A76 1987   404'.2   87–1524
  ISBN 0–905028–71–6
  ISBN 0–905028–70–8 (pbk.)

British Library Cataloguing in Publication Data

Arnberg, Lenore
  Raising children bilingually: the pre-
  school years. – (Multilingual matters; 29)
  I. Bilingualism in children
  I. Title   II. Series
  404'.2'0880543   P115

  ISBN 0–905028–71–6
  ISBN 0–905028–70–8 Pbk

Multilingual Matters Ltd
Bank House, 8a Hill Road,
Clevedon, Avon BS21 7HH,
England.

Typeset by Impression Typesetting, Bristol BS1 5LH
Cover designed by Julia Morland
Printed and bound in Great Britain by
Short Run Press Ltd., Exeter EX2 7LW.

This book is dedicated to parents and their endeavours to enrich their children's lives and deepen intercultural understanding.

Contents

Foreword

Joshua A. Fishman
Yeshiva University,
New York, N.Y.

Arnberg's delightful treatment of the pains and pleasures of raising children bilingually is not the first book on this topic for parents whose mother tongues differ from the surrounding majority language. A few years ago (1982), Multilingual Matters also published George Saunders' *Bilingual Children: Guidance for the Family*. Even that work was not the very first of its kind, since several linguists had published accounts of how their children had fared when, for years, mother had spoken one language to them and father, another. However, Saunders' was the first "how to do it" guide for a certain type of bilingual family, indicating that this type was becoming sufficiently numerous and widespread to receive explicit attention and assistance. Indeed, the *Bilingual Family Newletter,* also edited by Saunders and published by Multilingual Matters, has rendered yeoman's service in this very connection and has become an indispensable instrument for catharsis, information exchange and motivational reinforcement for all those who are involved in "bilingual families of the first kind". That this type of multilingual family is beginning to get at least some of the attention it deserves is itself a very noteworthy indication of a Zeitgeist that values bilingualism and that tries to cultivate it, at least in middle-class children fortunate enough to be blessed by it. That, indeed, is an often mentioned and relatively new "fact of life" with respect to "bilingual families of the first kind": they are frequently constituted by adults who are well educated, often associated with academic, consular, school teacher or other highly literate and professional or semi-professional social strata. Typically, only one adult member of these families has mastered a language other than that most current in the environment and it is this language that these families seek to perpetuate in their children. That such families should value bilingualism in their children, rather than seek to avoid or escape from it, as is regrettably so often the case among less fortunate families, is the continuation of an approach of very ancient vintage, an approach that is in full agreement with the admonition that "to them that hath shall be given".

However, there are at least two other kinds of bilingual families and Arnberg's book is directed toward these as well: to "bilingual families of the second kind". Families of this kind are immigrant derived and, in contrast to "bilingual families of the first kind" they constitute a minority culture within their host countries, i.e., they correspond to neighborhoods and communities of their own and, quite commonly, support institutions of their own (schools, places of worship, periodical publications, etc.) via which their own language and culture can be fostered on a societal basis. Bilingual children growing up in families of both of the types that we have mentioned thus far may have bilingual families but these families differ from one type to the other. In "bilingual families of the second type" both parents commonly speak the same language to their children but this language is immigrant-derived, the parents themselves usually being newcomers to their current country of origin. Thus, while the societal basis of "bilingual families of the second kind" doubtlessly strengthens such families and makes it easier for them to hand on to their children a language which is not common in the general environment (a societal prop for family bilingualism that many "bilingual families of the first kind" lack, either entirely or in part, and often wish they could have), their immigrant status is often a handicap, socially, economically and, at times, legally as well.

Another type of bilingual family is that which pertains to indigenous minorities. These "bilingual families of the third kind" did not come from some place else, at least not in recent generations. They are living in their own ancestral homes, but in the country at large they are a minority. The Swedes in Finland, the Frisians in The Netherlands, the Sorbs in East Germany, the Hungarians in Rumania, Orthodox Yiddish speaking Jews in Israel, White Russians (and members of hosts of other non-Russian nationalities) in the USSR, Armenians in Egypt, Anglophones in Quebec, these are all examples of "bilingual families of the third kind". Their efforts to attain inter-generational ethnolinguistic continuity, while at the same time making sure that their children also master the general language of the country or province in which they reside, makes childhood bilingualism a recurring experience for them. They commonly have a stronger claim to constitutional protection and to educational reinforcement of their bilingual goals than do the immigrant derived "bilingual families of the second kind", but even for "bilingual families of the third kind" their first steps along the path toward these goals must be taken at home, in the bosom of the family.

Clearly, it is the initial family context that is the common feature for bilingual children of all kinds. Fortunately, this is the very context that Arnberg stresses. That is why the core of her book should be of such great interest to all bilingual families, regardless of which type they happen to be. Old and new questions are answered, numerous tips are given on what to do, how to do it and when to do it, examples of successful practice abound, and, above all, an informed air of quiet confidence prevails, even in connection with choosing between difficult alternatives. This is an enjoyable and well-informed book and that is a combination that is hard to beat. It should be extremely useful for all good friends of bilingual children, not just for the parents but for the grandparents, the aunts, uncles and cousins, the neighbours and teachers and well-wishers alike. "Raising Children Bilingually: The Pre-School Years" is a book whose time has come. I welcome it and wish it well and will refer to it often in conjunction with my own bilingual grandchildren. It may not have been written especially for them, but, as will most other readers of this wonderful little book, I kept thinking that it was written especially for the particular bilingual children who are closest to my heart. I feel indebted to Arnberg, and, I am sure, so will all others who read this book, whether they do so for practical or theoretical reasons.

Acknowledgements

A number of people have been instrumental in shaping this book. I would first like to thank my husband, Peter, for his interest and support throughout the project and for his many valuable comments on the manuscript. I am also indebted to the following for their comments on earlier drafts: Barry McLaughlin, University of California, Stanislav Dornic, Stockholm University, Ragnhild Söderbergh, Lund University, and Marilyn Vihman, Stanford University. My colleagues at the Bilingualism Research Unit have provided valuable criticism on earlier drafts, and I would especially like to thank Kenneth Hyltenstam, Christopher Stround, Björn Hammerberg, and Suzanne Schlyter. Other colleagues who I would like to thank are Kerstin Nauclér, Leena Huss, Eva Eckerbrant-Cantillo and Jane Summerton.

The writing of this book has, in part, been made possible by a grant from the Swedish Delegation for Social Research and I am grateful to Inga-Britta Astedt and Merike Lidholm for their support of the project.

Thanks are due to Harcourt Brace Jovanovich, Inc. for permission to reprint the diagram from *Psychology and Language* by Herbert H. Clark and Eve V. Clark.

Finally, although it is impossible to mention them by name, I would like to thank the many parents and children who, in raising or being raised bilingually have, over the years, convinced me of the need for writing this book and provided much of the material which it contains.

PART I:
Background

1 Introduction

There are a number of different reasons why children become bilingual. For many people growing up in predominantly monolingual countries, bilingualism represents the exception rather than the rule. It is important to realize, however, that bilingualism is present in some form in nearly all countries throughout the world. Thus, for many children it is as natural to grow up speaking more than one language as it is to grow up speaking only one. More recently, however, the area of childhood bilingualism has received increasing attention as changing patterns in world mobility have resulted in more and more parents raising their children in a foreign country. This may occur not only in families consisting of married couples from the same country or single immigrant/minority group parents but also in mixed-language families where one or even both the parents are foreigners (in the latter case from two different countries). This may be the result of factors such as travelling, studying, or working abroad, intermarriage, or being forced to leave one's own country for political, economic or religious reasons. As a result, millions of children the world over are exposed to two or sometimes even three or four languages at an early age. A third source of bilingualism is the increased interest in foreign language learning among majority language parents as nations become increasingly interdependent and it becomes more and more of an asset to know more than one language. Many such parents place their children in so-called immersion programmes from an early age, this resulting in a high degree of proficiency in the foreign language for their children. One of the best-documented examples of such programmes are the French-medium schools in Canada for English-speaking children.

With regard to child bilingualism in all three of the above areas, however, (i.e. in the "bilingual country", as a result of immigration, and as a result of foreign language learning) the main focus has been on bilingualism in the school setting. In contrast, rather little attention has been paid to the question of bilingualism in the home and to the important role which parents play in children's learning of two languages. The aim of this book is to begin to fill some of the information needs existing in this area.

There is much evidence suggesting that many parents may experience difficulties when faced with the task of raising their children bilingually. Some of these difficulties are poignantly described in the following letter which I recently received from an immigrant mother. (Details in the letter have been changed in order to protect the identity of the parent):

Letter from an immigrant mother

I noticed your announcement in the Immigrant Newsletter and it was exactly what I've been looking for for months now. I have been unable to find anyone who can answer my questions, give me advice, or simply understand what it is that I find so difficult.

It may perhaps seem ridiculous, but I am beginning to experience a sense of despair with regard to the language contact between myself and my two-and-a-half-year-old daughter. I feel that instead of growing closer to each other we are growing further and further apart every day. You, perhaps, may think that one cannot expect so much from such a young child. But my feelings concern the future much more than the present situation.

Let me describe our situation. I am a Polish immigrant who has been living in Sweden for approximately five years. My husband is Swedish and does not know any Polish. Anna, our only child, is nearly two-and-a-half and it is she whom this letter concerns. My most urgent question (and that which the whole problem is based on) is the following: Is it really possible for my daughter to learn Polish at home in the circumstances in which we live?

It is my strongest wish that my daughter and I be able to communicate with each other in my language. My husband as well as everyone else is also highly positive toward my raising my daughter bilingually and would like to help, if they only could. But the entire environment (i.e. father, day nursery, grandparents, cousins, neighbours, etc.) speak only Swedish. We live in a residential area in which there are very few immigrant families and we have hardly any contact with other Poles.

My daughter is beginning to speak a great deal now and more and more is happening in her language development every day. I feel that she is both a lively and an intelligent child. But no matter how much I try to speak Polish with her, the pattern is the same. When she and I are alone together I speak only Polish to her. I try to speak as much as possible about what we are doing, describing things in the environment, explaining pictures we look at in books, sing, etc. This is not always easy for me as I really don't like to talk a lot. But no matter what I do, Anna answers in Swedish, questions me in Swedish, etc. I stubbornly try to repeat her little sentences in Polish and answer her in Polish.

I do this because it is nearly the only contact she has with the language. But at the same time I find this so exhausting – and unnatural! OK, she seems to understand most of what I'm saying. But out of her flows Swedish and Swedish and Swedish!

When she and I are together with her father, grandparents, at her day nursery, or with friends (all Swedish) it becomes natural for me to also address Anna in Swedish. I have great difficulty speaking Polish to her during these occasions, i.e. speaking a totally incomprehensible language in front of others. This feels wrong to me, impolite, and, frankly, impossible. In the beginning when I was trying to be extremely consistent in speaking Polish, I tried to do this even in front of Swedes. But this ended up in my becoming completely silent after one or two words. So I began doing what felt most natural to me, i.e. speaking Swedish with my daughter when Swedes were present. Was I wrong?

Now I feel that Anna understands me less and less (and that she cares less and less what I have to say altogether) and I need some sensible advice about all of this – either some encouragement plus some practical suggestions or simply being told to give up,that raising a child bilingually just won't work in our situation.

All of this is so enormously important to me right now because it influences one's entire life. So much in our relationships with other people is based on language. I am beginning to feel impatient, irritated and so extremely tired . . . . . at not seeing any positive results of all my efforts, plus forcing myself not to give up. Can you please give me some advice as to what I should do? Can Anna learn to speak Polish from me? When do children normally begin to show signs of being bilingual? Should I force myself to speak only Polish to her, even in front of Swedes?

I sincerely hope that you will find the time to respond to this letter.

This mother is not alone. I have received many other letters from parents over the years expressing similar concerns. Many of the issues taken up in this letter will be addressed in various parts of the book, but I would like to begin by giving a reasurring affirmative answer (as was sent to the above mother), that, yes, I do feel that it is possible to raise a child bilingually in the situation described above. Nevertheless, at the same time, parents may need to be aware of the importance of seeing their children's bilingualism in a long-term rather than a short-term perspective. They must also be realistic about what degrees of bilingualism are possible to achieve in various family situations.

Some of the specific issues addressed in the letter which will be taken up in the book are the following:

- forming realistic expectations about what can be achieved in various family situations (Chapters 4 & 8);
- whether or not it is important to be consistent when speaking the minority language to the child (Chapter 7);
- the importance of having long-range goals when raising children bilingually (Chapter 8);
- the value of continuing to speak the minority language although the child may not "answer back" in this language (Chapters 7 & 8);
- ways of supporting language development in the minority language both in- and outside the home (Chapters 9 & 10).

Thus, although it is probably correct to state that *all* parents could benefit from increased information about their children's language development and how to support it in the home, immigrant/minority group parents may especially be in need of such information. There are several reasons why this may be so, and I would like to conclude this chapter with a brief discussion of these.

Why write a book about raising children bilingually?

Before discussing reasons for writing a book about raising children bilingually, let me begin by briefly describing my background for my readers. I myself am an immigrant from the United States and have lived in Sweden for the past twelve years. I was also acquainted with the many aspects of being an immigrant long before that as I was a third generation immigrant in the United States.

I first became interested in bilingualism through my own learning of Swedish as an adult and this interest gradually increased to include bilingualism in pre-school age children. In 1981 I completed a doctoral dissertation having the title, *Early Childhood Bilingualism in the Mixed-Lingual Family*, in which children learning two languages in the home were studied. Since that time I have continued to have many contacts with bilingual families and to carry out research and teaching in the area of child bilingualism with a special focus on the role of families in the child's learning of two languages. Along with these activities I have also had the opportunity to visit the United States, Australia, England and Wales in order to learn about bilingualism in these countries. Throughout these activities a number of aspects about the particular situation of immigrant/minority group parents raising their children bilingually have caught my attention and impressed me with the need for writing this book. These include the following:

Raising children bilingually is difficult

Firstly, raising children bilingually is not an easy task. Many parents are unprepared for this fact and when the expected positive results are not achieved, they may place the blame on themselves or on their children. As a consequence of the difficulties experienced, many may even give up their attempts to raise their children bilingually altogether. Thus, one purpose of this book is to describe the results from other families so that parents will be prepared for some of the difficulties which may arise. Many parents find support in knowing that other parents have experienced similar problems in raising their children bilingually and have overcome these. With this knowledge in mind they may be encouraged to continue in their efforts if the going gets rough.

Of course, it must also be recognized that some parents, for one reason or another, may decide that they do not wish to raise their children bilingually. Perhaps it is the case that the parents are highly fluent in the majority language, plan to remain permanently in the new country and see no particular reason for teaching the child the minority language. Such decisions must, of course, be respected. Nevertheless, the failure to raise one's child bilingually should be based on such a choice, i.e. not occur because of a failure to receive necessary information. This is because it is my firm conviction that most immigrant parents would like their children to become bilingual. Many parents feel that communication with their children is impaired when the majority language is used. Also, parents feel that, as a result of knowing the minority language, the child will become familiar with its social and cultural heritage, be able to communicate with grandparents (who may be monolingual), etc. Furthermore, most parents recognize the many advantages associated with bilingualism, e.g. in working life or in learning to know and understand the peoples of other cultures and naturally, wish to pass these on to their children.

Thus, the first goal of this book is to prepare parents for the task at hand by describing some of the problems which they may encounter along the way.

Bilingual families have many choices open to them

Secondly, the number of alternatives open to bilingual parents regarding language choice (i.e. how the two languages are to be used in the home and outer environment) is simply greater than it is for the majority language family. Majority language parents do not normally need to ask themselves which language they will speak to their children or in what language the child will be educated because, at least in most cases, these decisions are clear. There are, of course, some majority parents who will be faced with the issue of whether or not to place their children in a foreign language immersion programme, and these parents face similar choices to those of the bilingual family. For the bilingual family, however, the choice of which language(s) is/are to be used in the home and in the child's schooling is a far more complicated issue.

Thus, the second goal of this book is to discuss the various alternatives which are open to parents as well as what is known about their effects.

Information available to parents is confusing

Thirdly, information available to parents about raising their children bilingually is confusing at the present time. Research findings give no clear-cut answers concerning the pros and cons of early bilingualism and have often resulted in a polarization of opinions in the area. Parents often become caught in the middle of the various opinions about bilingualism, e.g. when they consult professionals about their concerns in raising their children bilingually, read articles about bilingualism in the newspaper, etc. Although well-meaning in their attempts to guide parents, various professionals are, understandably, not always aware of the complexity of the issues involved or well-read concerning the latest research findings. And even those parents who are motivated to read research findings on their own and try to find direct answers to their questions can easily become overwhelmed by the sheer amount of material available or by the difficulty of reading research reports which are often not written with the layman in mind.

Thus, a third goal of this book is to present objective and current information about bilingualism in a non-technical manner so that parents themselves can evaluate the available knowledge in the field and make decisions which reflect their own needs and situations.

Immigrant/minority group parents are important "teachers" of their children

Another reason why immigrant/minority group parents are especially in need of information is because of the vital role they play in their children's development in the minority language and culture. In contrast to the majority language child who has many sources of language and cultural input, for the minority language child the parents may represent the major or only source of input which the child receives. Even when parents are fortunate enough to be assisted by bilingual education programmes, they simply cannot assume that the pre-school or school can do the whole job. This fact was pointed out in a recent research report investigating the effects which schools *and* parents have on maintaining the minority language in the United States in which the following was stated:

> "The primary responsibility for inter-generational ethnic language maintenance rests squarely with the parents in their domain – the family. Delegating this primary responsibility to others amounts to substituting unrealistic hope (in the public schools) for practical control (of the family) – and the loss of the linguistic heritage" (Kjolseth, 1982: 25).

Thus, if parents are to support their children in becoming bilingual they must be given information about how they can best stimulate their children's language development in the minority language.

Thus, a fourth goal of this book is to give practical suggestions for encouraging the use of the minority language both in- and outside the home which can be used by parents.

Bilingualism is important

A final reason for writing this book is because, if I may be allowed to express my own personal bias for a moment, I feel that bilingualism is important, not only for the individual child and family but for the entire society. This was expressed very eloquently at a lecture I attended several years ago at an American University in which the speaker, a United States congressman, expressed deep concern about the lack of interest in learning foreign languages in the United States.

Three reasons were mentioned why bilingualism is important at the societal level. Firstly, bilingualism is broadening for the citizens of a country, leading to less provincial attitudes which are also likely to be reflected in the leaders who are chosen for the country. Secondly, bilingualism is important for economic reasons. The speaker cited examples of millions of dollars being needlessly wasted each year because of terrible translations. Finally, bilingualism is important for international relations. In our current world situation, it is vital that nations are able to understand and empathize with one another and this can best be accomplished, e.g. in disarmament talks, when participants have a direct understanding of one another's languages and cultures.

Bilingualism is also advantageous at the individual level. One might suggest that bilingualism opens up possibilities for the individual, giving the bilingual and bicultural person a wider range of options than the monolingual and monocultural person has, such as the opportunity to live and work in another country or to learn to know the people of another country on an intimate basis. Many parents also mention the broadening effects which they feel that bilingualism has on their children's thinking as a result of a wider access to ideas and experiences and the enriching experience of being exposed to two cultures than would have been the case had the child been monolingual.

Thus, in short, it is felt that support and encouragement be given to parents who have an excellent opportunity to cultivate a resource which is of value to the individual, family and society. It is also important that parents receive information as early as possible in their children's lives as, for a number of reasons which will be discussed in various sections of this book, it is felt that the pre-school years are one of the best times of all in which to become bilingual.

For which "parents" is the present book intended?

Parents raising children bilingually can fall into a number of different categories. These include the following:

- immigrant or minority group parents where the parents share a similar language background;
- single parent immigrant/minority group families;
- mixed-lingual families where one parent comes from an immigrant or minority group background and the other comes from a majority group background;
- mixed-lingual families where the parents represent two *different* language and cultural backgrounds;
- majority language parents wishing to educate their children in another language.

Obviously, it is difficult to write a book for *all* of the above groups. My strategy has thus been to focus mainly on the needs of the immigrant or minority group family although certain chapters such as those concerning the effects of bilingualism (Chapter 3) and simultaneous and successive bilingualism (Chapter 6) will also be of interest to majority group parents. With regard to immigrant and minority group families, I have attempted to provide information which will be useful both to the "homogeneous" family as well as to the mixed-lingual family. Certain chapters, however, e.g. concerning language strategies in the bilingual family (Chapter 7), will primarily be of interest to the mixed-lingual family. Recently, attention has been increasingly drawn to family trilingualism. The reason why this topic has not been dealt with specifically in the present book is not due to a lack of interest, but rather to a lack of information. Thus, information about family trilingualism will also be presented when it is available, but otherwise it will be assumed that information on family bilingualism, at least to some extent, is also applicable to a trilingual situation.

2 Immigrant parents

Raising children bilingually starts with parents

Although the present book is about raising children bilingually any discussion of this topic must begin with the parents themselves. Answers to questions such as why the parents have emigrated to begin with; whether they plan to remain in the new country and, if so, for how long; how their present living situation is; to what extent they consider it important to maintain ties with the native language and culture; and how they feel about living in the new country, are likely to have an important influence on their attitudes towards, and their motivation for, raising their children bilingually.

Ways in which emigration may influence children's bilingualism

As any psychologist is fully aware, parents' life situation has an important influence on their child's development. Although emigrating to a new country as an adult is felt to result in an identity crisis for all immigrants it is clear that the gravity of the crisis, as well as the means for coping with it, differs greatly from individual to individual. For some immigrants the cultures and ways of life in the old and new countries are highly similar; moreover, the emigration may have been of an entirely voluntary nature. For others, however, the emigration may have been more or less forced and may represent a confrontation with an entirely new culture and value system. In the current life cycles of some immigrant families, it may thus be difficult to give priority to issues such as children's language development when other problems appear much more pressing. In such circumstances there may be nothing to do but to eliminate the source of stress before parents have the necessary energy to devote to their children's growth and development. Although such issues are fully understood, it will not be possible to consider them in more depth in the present book which has mainly an educational focus.

Another way in which emigration may influence children's language development and subsequent bilingualism is related to the breaking down of the social network which was a source of language and cultural input in the native country. After emigrating to a new country, relatives may be geographically isolated from one another, and social interactions which may earlier have been carried out through face-to-face contact on a daily or regular basis may now be carried out by other means, such as the telephone. This, of course, has a negative influence on children's exposure to the minority language and parents should do what they can to maintain contact with others in ways that foster the child's language and cultural growth.

Finally, although rather little is known about this issue, parents emigrating to a new country may want to be aware of research findings suggesting that children of certain ages may be particularly sensitive to a shift from a monolingual to a bilingual environment. The period of one to three years (i.e. 12 to 36 months) has been found to be a particularly sensitive one in contrast to earlier and later ages. Such issues may be important to consider when choosing what type of day care programme in which to place the child (see Chapter 6).

Parents are models for their children's behaviour

Parents' attitudes toward bilingualism are also important in a more indirect way. Because parents are models for their children, their attitudes and behaviour are often imitated by their children. Thus, if parents show that it is a useful and a positive thing to know two languages and to belong to two cultural groups this will help their children to develop similar positive attitudes. If, on the other hand, parents are negative toward one of the language and cultural groups this may in turn make it difficult for their children to see the benefits of being bilingual and bicultural.

Different ways of adjusting to a new culture

Becoming a "good bilingual and bicultural model" is of course not an easy task and one which may require many years. It is a difficult thing to move to a new country and learn a new language as an adult. François Grosjean in his comprehensive book on bilingualism (see "Suggestions for Further Reading") suggests that there are a number of ways in which adults may adjust to a new culture. Some individuals may *isolate* themselves and never adjust. This may be the case for the elderly or for those who plan to remain only a short time in the new country and, thus, do not wish to make the effort it takes to learn a new language and adjust to a new culture. It may, unfortunately, also sometimes be the case that immigrants are not allowed to adjust to the new country by members of the majority group. A second pattern may be that of *over-adjustment*. In this case the person tries to adopt the values and behaviour patterns of members of the majority group, rejecting everything which has to do with his/her own group. In neither of the above cases, however, can one really talk about a high degree of bilingualism and biculturalism. Rather, the individual has chosen to identify more strongly with one group or the other.

Between the two extremes, however, may be various degrees of biculturalism where the individual keeps some aspects of the native language and culture while, at the same time, adopting some aspects of the new language and culture. This process has been called *integration*. Although integration must be seen as the most positive way of coping with one's bilingual and bicultural status, it is not without its problems. For example, one problem with integration can be that it may lead to a person feeling that he/she does not really belong to either group, i.e. the feeling of being a "marginal" person. This feeling is sometimes referred to as "anomie".

Anomie

Anomie is a feeling of disorientation, social isolation and anxiety. It does not appear in the beginning stages of learning a new language and adjusting to a new culture but tends to appear when the individual has made good progress in the new language, i.e. at the point where he/she moves out of one linguistic and cultural group into the other. A problem which is sometimes claimed in connection with the bilingual and bicultural person is that the "new" group begins to expect more and more in the way of conformity in behaviour patterns as more progress is made in learning the new language. At the same time, however, the immigrant's native language group (e.g. friends and relatives in the minority language country) expect the person to behave as if he had not assimilated any of the values of the new group. This dilemma has been described in the following way by some researchers:

> "... it is difficult to be both Jewish and Russian, or Algerian and French, and this is so because the person involved realizes that two separate networks of valued people expect him to show unambiguous signs of allegiance to one group or the other. It is extremely painful to be caught in the influence systems of two or more ethnic groups and to be 'tested' by members of one group or the other who demand evidence of one's true colors" (Lambert, Giles & Picard, 1975: 127).

It is important to point out, however, that "being caught between two ethnic groups" need not only have negative effects. In a recent Swedish study of 48 immigrants from different countries who had come to Sweden as adults, although 71% of those interviewed admitted to feelings of "not really feeling completely at home in either country" (many immigrants feel that they grow away from their native countries due to changes in themselves or in the country itself during their absence), this was not necessarily seen as negative. Many of the interviewees stated that they found it an asset, leading to greater independence, a more cosmopolitan attitude and lifestyle, and personal growth. Also, although this feeling will undoubtedly remain in varying degrees with most of the immigrants interviewed throughout their lives, many suggested that it was simply something "one learned to live with".

Ways of coping

One way in which many immigrants find their way out of this dilemma is by identifying with others who are in a similar situation, i.e. with other so-called hyphenated Americans (e.g. Franco-Americans, Hispanic Americans), Australians, etc. It is extremely important for immigrants to have the opportunity to meet with others from their own group in order to discuss feelings in connection with adjustment to the new country. As to my own immigrant adjustment in Sweden, I have found the following organizations and activities helpful:

- discussions with other immigrant women within the context of international immigrant women's organizations;
- monthly meetings with other women sharing my own immigrant background for discussions, literature circles about current American and British literature, etc.;
- various immigrant clubs and organizations with regard to both my own immigrant group and other immigrant groups.

This, of course, does not mean that one should associate only with members of one's own ethnic group; contact with the majority group is equally important. For example, parents should make an attempt to learn the majority language as well as possible, not only for their own sakes but also for their children's. Although this, of course, does not mean that the majority language need be spoken in the home, the parents' knowledge of the majority language will help them to provide opportunities for their children to learn this language and enable them to understand what is going on in their children's lives. It is also the case that one is naturally afraid of the unknown. If one has not learned anything about the new language and way of life, one may, although unconsciously, hinder one's children in their bilingual and bicultural development.

It is very important that parents resolve issues related to their own linguistic and cultural identity so that conflicts in this area do not influence their children's bilingual and bicultural development. A serious problem for many immigrant parents is that children often adjust to the new culture and language more quickly than their parents do, causing many parents to feel that they are losing contact with their children. Although this is certainly a most difficult situation and there are no easy solutions, these feelings must also be discussed and resolved in some way.

The importance of the parents' positive bilingual and bicultural development for their children's development

In many ways the situation for the children of immigrant parents is even more complex. Although the parents can always fall back on their own cultural group, children may experience an enormous conflict of loyalties between the attitudes, values and behaviour patterns of their peers in the majority group and those of the parents. Although the parents may be on their way toward becoming more and more bilingual and bicultural they are likely to deviate strongly from majority group parents in their values and customs, be less familiar with the child's school and cultural world and, consequently, less able to help the child adjust to this world. Some studies have shown that minority group adolescents may experience difficulties in coping with their dual identities, many feeling forced to choose between one group or the other. It is highly important that the child be helped in developing a positive bilingual and bicultural identity during the pre-school years so that such identity problems during the teenage years can be avoided.

Choosing to identify with one group or the other, need not, of course, be the only way of resolving one's affiliation with two ethnic groups. In a Canadian study of teenage children from mixed English-French-speaking families it was found that the teenagers, when compared with a monolingual control group, showed a healthy adjustment. Rather than rejecting one group or the other, the children identified with both ethnic groups, showed no signs of personality disturbances or anxiety, and had positive relationships with both parents. One can question why these results were so positive in contrast to those from other studies. The answer to this question is undoubtedly related in part to the fact that both languages shared equal status as international languages as well as being official languages in Canada. Other reasons, however, were that the parents themselves were bilingual and bicultural and were highly supportive of these traits in their children.

Factors important in the development of a positive bilingual and bicultural identity in immigrant/minority group children

Although the present chapter focuses on the role of immigrant parents in their children's bilingual and bicultural development, I would like to conclude the chapter by focusing on the child. This is felt to be appropriate given the main goal of this book.

Although the above results with regard to the Canadian teenagers reflect a rather ideal situation they, nevertheless, suggest factors which are important if children are to positively identify with both of their languages and cultures. A positive environment for bilingual and bicultural adjustment is summed up in the following quotation:

"If the two cultures are valued equally in the home, in the school and in the society at large and if biculturalism is judged to be as valuable as monoculturalism, then children and adolescents who are in contact with two cultures will accept both instead of rejecting or being rejected by one or the other or by both." (Grosjean, 1982: 166).

In addition to the role of parents, the above quotation also emphasizes the role of the school and society in influencing children's attitudes, both directly and indirectly. The indirect influence has to do with the ways in which these areas influence parents. It is difficult for parents to develop positive attitudes towards bilingualism and biculturalism if they feel that their language and cultural group is not valued by members of the majority group. Attitudes at the school and societal level can also influence children in more direct ways, e.g. in the ways in which the minority language and culture are represented in the classroom, in curricular materials, in the mass media, etc. An important task for the future is thus to find ways of supporting bilingualism and biculturalism at all levels not only in the family but also in the pre-school and school, in various areas of working and professional life, and in society in general.

PART II:
Should I raise my child bilingually?

A major question facing many immigrant and minority group parents is whether or not they should raise their children bilingually in the first place. Here, questions such as what effects bilingualism has on the child's development, what degree of bilingualism it is possible to achieve in various family situations, and how much effort will be required of parents, are frequently raised. These questions will be focused on in Part II. In Parts III, IV, and V issues will be focused on which are related to *how* to go about raising one's child bilingually once the decision to do so has been made.

The first chapter in this section (Chapter 3) looks at the results from research studies on the effects of bilingualism on different areas of the child's development. In Chapter 4, research findings looking at what level of proficiency in the minority language can be achieved in the situation of the bilingual family are focused on. The issue of how much effort is required of parents in raising children bilingually is also mentioned. However, this topic will be discussed more thoroughly in Chapter 8.

3 The effects of bilingualism on the child's development

Many parents worry that bilingualism may have a negative effect on their children's development and questions about the "side effects" of bilingualism are often raised. Parents also question whether bilingualism may not even have a positive effect on certain aspects of their children's development. This chapter will briefly summarize research findings concerning what is known about both the positive and negative effects of bilingualism. The effects of bilingualism on the following areas, among others, have been studied by researchers:

intelligence;
cognitive development;
language development;
social development.

Bilingualism and intelligence

The study of the effects of bilingualism on intelligence has long interested psychologists and educators. The earliest study was carried out in Wales in 1923. Many of the studies have had serious weaknesses from a research point of view, however, thus making it difficult to find any clear-cut evidence for either positive or negative effects of bilingualism on intellectual development at the present time.

Before 1960, research results often showed a negative relation between bilingualism and intelligence. In measuring intelligence one can either use verbal or non-verbal tests, and this result was especially evident when verbal intelligence tests were used. These studies were often poorly controlled, however. In order to study whether bilingualism itself is the cause of poor test results one must be careful to match bilingual and monolingual children on all other characteristics. This was often not done, however, and, thus, there is no way of knowing whether it was bilingualism or other factors such as social background which led to the poor test results. Another problem was that often no attempt was made to determine exactly how bilingual the children were. This meant that some of the children may have had only limited contact with the language of the test beforehand. And even if the child does possess knowledge of certain words, idioms, and grammatical patterns in the second language, he/she may be handicapped in the sense of not knowing the language well enough to use it as a tool for thinking and problem solving. Thus, the earlier results do not necessarily show that bilingual children were inferior to monolingual children in verbal intelligence but, rather, that they may have had a language handicap when tested in their weaker language.

Studies after 1960, which in general have been better controlled, have tended to show more positive effects of bilingualism. In a landmark study in Canada in 1962 by Elizabeth Peal and Wallace Lambert it was even found that French-English-speaking bilingual children performed *better* on both verbal and non-verbal intelligence tests than a group of French-speaking monolingual children. Other Canadian studies of immersion students (i.e. children who attend schools in which all instruction is carried out through the medium of a second language) have shown similar positive effects.

These studies finding positive effects have also been criticized on methodological grounds, however. In an attempt to overcome some of the weaknesses of earlier studies such as the lack of control for degree of bilingualism, the researchers often used very strict definitions of bilingualism. This often had the effect of disqualifying many children from participation in the studies because they were not "bilingual enough". This situation has caused a number of researchers to suggest that in order to achieve such a high degree of bilingualism, some degree of intelligence is probably necessary. Thus, the difference between the monolingual and bilingual children in intelligence test scores in many of the "positive" studies could be because the bilingual children were more intelligent to begin with!

It is also important to realize that studies finding positive effects and those finding negative effects have been carried out on children from very different backgrounds. In general, the positive effects are associated with settings where the children represent the majority group, where attitudes among those such as teachers have been highly positive towards the children's first language, where the children come from middle-class backgrounds and where bilingualism has been a choice rather than a necessity. Negative effects, on the other hand, have often been associated with settings where children represent a minority group, where attitudes among majority group members such as teachers have been negative or at least ambivalent towards the minority language, where the children come from working-class backgrounds, and where bilingualism has not been a choice but a necessity. According to many researchers it is probably differences such as these rather than bilingualism as such which have contributed to the contradictory research findings.

Thus, at present, there are no studies which have convincingly shown that bilingualism has either a positive or a negative effect on children's intellectual development. Furthermore, it is questionable whether this issue will be able to be settled with the research methods that are being used now. One important reason for this is that children have not been randomly assigned to the bilingual or monolingual groups; instead the situation is such that some parents have chosen to place their children in a bilingual programme whereas others have not. This means that even if the children are matched on many relevant characteristics there may still be differences between the groups, e.g. with regard to parental attitudes toward bilingualism. Unless true experiments are carried out where children are randomly assigned to the bilingual and monolingual groups we cannot obtain a clear picture of exactly which factors are causing the results. It is, of course, unlikely that this problem will be able to be solved due to the difficulty of telling parents whether or not they should educate their children bilingually. The only other alternative in this situation is to match the children initially on as many characteristics as possible and then test them at different points in time instead of only once as is usually the case. Although this does not eliminate the possibility of there being factors which have not been controlled for, it at least gives a fuller picture of how a bilingual or monolingual experience influences the child. Few studies have been carried out using such long range research designs. In one study using such a design, however, no difference was found between bilingual and monolingual children on intelligence test measures.

Bilingualism and cognitive development

More recent studies have shifted away from looking at the effects of bilingualism on intelligence tests to measuring whether bilingualism influences the child's cognitive development. By cognitive development is meant how certain "higher mental processes" such as knowledge, thinking, problem-solving ability, conceptualization, symbolization, etc. develop in the child. There are several reasons why researchers have shifted to this focus of interest.

One reason has been an increased interest in the *nature* of the effects of bilingualism on intelligence rather than simply whether or not it has a positive or a negative effect. Another reason was some interesting observations by a researcher named Werner Leopold. Leopold, a professor of German at an American university, carried out a study which is perhaps the most extensive investigation of a bilingual child to this day. In a four-volume work he described the bilingual development of his daughter, Hildegard, raised bilingually in German and English from birth. From observations of his daughter, Leopold suggested that by continually hearing objects and events referred to by two names (i.e. two different phonetic forms) the bilingual child realizes at an early age that the relationship between a word's sound and its meaning is an arbitrary one. In this way the bilingual child is felt to focus on the essential aspects of objects at an earlier age than the monolingual child does, this realization being essential for the child's cognitive development. Other explanations have also been given why bilingualism may positively influence cognitive development, for example, the enriching experience of being exposed to two cultures or the development of a flexible attitude as a result of having to frequently switch between one's two languages.

A number of experiments have been carried out looking at whether bilingual children are earlier than monolinguals in learning to separate word sound from word meaning. In one of the most cited of these studies, South African bilingual and monolingual children were given three words, e.g. "cap", "can", and "hat". The children were asked to state which of the words were most alike. Bilingual children, at a much earlier age than monolinguals, chose the words "cap" and "hat", thus focusing on the words' meanings rather than their sounds. Bilingual children were also more likely than monolinguals to agree that words for names could be interchanged. This was also seen as evidence for the fact that bilingual children realize at an early stage that the relation between the sound of a word and its meaning is an arbitrary one. For example, bilingual children more often than monolinguals gave a positive answer to the question, "Can you call a dog 'cow' and a cow 'dog'?".

Although studies using similar methods have sometimes supported these results, in other cases they have not. As a result, some researchers have suggested that it seems premature to suggest that bilingualism has a positive influence on the child's cognitive development. Instead of seeing bilingualism as leading to a greater understanding of language on a deeper level, a more common view has been to see the bilingual child as being more sensitive to certain formal aspects of language than the monolingual child is, as a result of being exposed to two languages. For example, in some studies it has been found that bilingual children are better at detecting grammatical errors in sentences than monolingual children are.

Bilingualism and
language development

One of the most frequent questions asked by immigrant and minority group parents is whether bilingualism will have a negative effect on the child's language development. What parents often appear to be concerned about is whether bilingualism causes a delay in the child's learning to speak and whether bilingualism negatively influences the child's learning to speak and language. Parents also worry that the child will mix the languages or that learning two languages at the same time will be confusing. Another issue concerns what degree of proficiency in the minority language can be achieved in the bilingual family situation. This last issue will be discussed in the next chapter, however.

Does bilingualism cause a delay in learning to speak?

Few studies have actually looked at whether bilingualism causes a delay in learning to speak. Such studies would have to involve large groups of children due to the fact that even monolingual children vary greatly in the age at which they begin talking. In one study, however, Taylor (1974) suggested that bilingual children will not be delayed in the learning of their first words because such words are linked to concepts as memorized responses. However, they may be delayed at a slightly later age when there is normally a vocabulary spurt associated with the child's learning of the "label concept", i.e. the understanding that all concepts have names. This is felt to be due to the fact that bilingual children hear two labels for most concepts, this leading to a less systematic exposure to labels than is the case for monolingual children.

Taylor's ideas were tested by a group of Canadian researchers who studied 13 monolingual and 13 bilingual children between the ages of 17 and 42 months. As was predicted, there was no difference between the two groups with regard to when first words were used (at about 12 months for all of the children). The bilingual children performed worse in a vocabulary test in their dominant language, however, when compared with the monolinguals. The researchers did not feel that this had to do with a delay in learning the "label concept", however, but rather because the children lacked a variety of input in each language as a result of their being exposed to two languages. This explanation is supported by a number of other studies which have shown that if the vocabularies from both the bilingual's languages are added together, there is often no difference between bilingual and monolingual children in the number of words known.

Does bilingualism negatively influence the child's learning of the majority language?

With regard to the effects of bilingualism on language development in the majority language, both positive and negative effects have been found. According to a literature review by Jensen (1962) negative effects have included the following: a smaller active and passive vocabulary; a confused, mixed vocabulary; less complex sentences; and the misuse of idiomatic expressions. Many studies, however, have claimed that the alleged handicaps of bilingualism are non-existent, smaller than assumed, or that bilingualism might even have a positive influence on language development. These differences in findings are, at least in part, due to the fact that the studies were of varying quality, involved subjects from different social backgrounds and different ages, etc. It should also be recognized that many of the studies involved school-age children where the effects of "bilingualism" could as well have been "the effects of being instructed through the medium of a weaker language".

Nevertheless, a number of studies have shown that in vocabulary and in the acquisition of certain grammatical forms such as tense markers, negatives, and prepositions, monolinguals have performed better than bilinguals. The productions of bilinguals have not been found to be inferior in complexity or logic, however. That bilingualism might affect the speed of learning some of the formal aspects of the majority language does not seem to be an unreasonable assumption. Because the bilingual child may receive less exposure to each language, more time may be required to achieve a similar level to that of the monolingual child. In the future it would be desirable to specify under what conditions the languages were learned and at what ages the children had been tested, however. Many studies, for example, have suggested that the bilingual child eventually "catches up" with the monolingual child after increased exposure.

As will be seen in the next chapter, children from families where one of the parents speaks the majority language seem to show a normal language development in this language, at least by the time they begin school. Although this may be less true for children in families where neither of the parents speaks the majority language, even in such families, children's language proficiency in the majority language is often as good, provided that there are many opportunities for exposure to this language outside the home.

Language mixing, code switching, and interference

As will be seen in Chapter 6, language mixing is not a sign of "confusion" but is a natural stage in the bilingual child's learning to separate his/her two languages. Language mixing must also be distinguished from two other language behaviours appearing in the bilingual child, i.e. *code switching* and *interference*. A brief discussion of these phenomena follows.

Language mixing

Language mixing refers to the young child's mixing of both languages within the same utterance *before* the child is really aware of having two languages in its environment.

Code switching

Code switching, on the other hand, refers to a conscious and/or purposeful switching of the two languages. This may consist of either inserting a word of phrase from the other language within an utterance or switching languages at the sentence boundary. Researchers have identified a number of reasons for code switching, including the following:

– a lack of a vocabulary item in one of the languages;
– certain activities having been experienced in only one of the languages;
– certain concepts being easier to express in one of the languages;
– certain words being simpler, more salient, or more accessible in one of the languages;
– to clarify a misunderstanding;
– to create a certain communication effect;
– as a continuation of the last language used (i.e. "triggering effect");
– to emphasize a point;
– to express group solidarity;
– to exclude someone from the conversation.

Researchers still know rather little about how code switching ability develops in children or about which of the above factors seem important among children of different ages.

Notice in the above list that, except for the last example, code switching requires that one's communication partner understands both languages. If a word from the wrong language is used when speaking to a monolingual speaker, this is usually due to interference, i.e. the speaker is not aware that the word used does not belong to the language being spoken. This is because it is assumed to be unnatural to speak to a person in a language which they do not understand. Of course, this may occur at times, e.g. a second language learner may "test" whether a word belongs to the language being spoken, be tired or stressed, etc.

Interference

Interference, then, is the involuntary influence of one language on the other which, like code switching, occurs after the child is aware of having two languages in its environment. Interference appears to be most frequent when the languages are out of balance. Many immigrant and minority group children show interference in the minority language due to the fact that the majority language is their dominant language. Interference in the opposite direction, i.e. from the minority to the majority language, although it occurs, especially while the child is in the process of learning the majority language, is less common. It should be recognized by parents that interference is not the only cause of errors in the minority language. Although the effect of one language dominating another means that certain patterns in the stronger language may influence those in the weaker language (i.e. interference), it also means that there will be less opportunity to use the weaker language, resulting in a slower development in this language. Some of the child's errors may thus reflect this slower development and be similar to those made by monolingual children learning to speak the language as their first language. Although in the case of the monolingual child these mistakes will gradually disappear, in the case of the bilingual child many will be harder to eliminate because the exposure to the language in the environment is limited.

Likewise, many research studies have shown that if the bilingual child spends an extended period of time in the minority language country, many of the child's errors disappear.

Interference occurs at all levels of language. Following is a brief description of different types of interference with examples taken from the speech of English-Swedish-speaking bilingual children growing up in Sweden. The examples are taken from the children's minority language, i.e. English.

Pronunciation: In pronunciation the child may appear to have an "accent" when speaking the minority language. Certain sounds in the minority language may be replaced by sounds in the majority language, especially when these are easier to pronounce in that language. An example is English-Swedish-speaking children's pronunciation of the expression "sleep well" as "sleep vell".

Words and idiomatic expressions: At the word level, words may be borrowed from the dominant language and adapted to the minority language. Examples are English-Swedish-speaking children's use of the Swedish words "matt" and "knapp" (adapted in pronunciation and form) for "rug" and "button" in English.

A more common interference error at the word level, however, is extending the meaning of a word which already exists in the minority language, to cover part of the meaning of a word in the majority language which has a similar spelling and pronunciation. An example is English-Swedish bilingual children's use of the word "house" to include "apartment buildings" as the similar Swedish word "hus" does.

Interference may also occur at the level of idiomatic expressions which may be translated directly from one language to the other as in the following utterances produced by English-Swedish-speaking pre-school children:

> How much is the clock? (from "Hur mycket är klockan?" instead of "What time is it?");
> What is there for food today? (from "Vad är det för mat idag?" instead of "What is for lunch today?").

Sentence level: At the sentence level word order patterns may be transferred from one language to the other as in the following examples:

> Where is now the nose (from "Var är nu näsan?" instead of "Where is the nose now?");
> Must take down that (from "Måste ta ner den" instead of "Must take that down").

Although the above description of language mixing, code switching and interference will give parents some insight into the types of "deviations" which occur in their children's speech, it should be realized that this is a highly simplified account. Researchers are not always in agreement concerning the definitions of the various terms, especially when these are used to describe children's speech, this making it sometimes difficult to distinguish the various behaviours from one another.

Are language mixing, code switching and interference "dangerous"?

Parents choosing not to raise their children bilingually because they worry about the effects of language mixing, code switching and interference would be hard pressed to find support for this position from research findings. Although language mixing is common in young children it seems to gradually disappear as the child learns to differentiate between the languages, and in most bilingual children it is rare beyond about the age of four. Furthermore, when looking at the child's total productions, language mixing appears in a rather small percentage of the child's utterances. This does not mean, however, that some children may not be delayed in learning to separate their languages or that parents have no role to play in this process. These issues will be further discussed in Chapter 6.

With regard to code switching, researchers have become increasingly sensitive to the fact that code switching requires skill in using two languages and is a natural communication strategy among persons who are familiar with two languages. Although many monolinguals and even some bilinguals have negative attitudes toward code switching, many bilinguals see it in a more positive light and consider it to be as effective a means of communication as monolingual speech. Nevertheless, code switching may be less positive when used by parents in front of young children, who are in the process of learning the two languages. This is because it may delay the child's learning to recognize which words belong to which language.

With regard to interference, parents should recognize the fact that interference has been shown to be difficult to avoid in situations where the languages are out of balance. Thus, rather than seeing interference as being "dangerous" or "confusing", parents should regard it as an inevitable consequence of a language situation where one language is more dominant than the other and help the child by increasing the exposure to the weaker language.

Bilingualism and social development

A number of studies have looked at the effects of bilingualism on the child's social development. Here again we have the problem of isolating the effects of bilingualism from the effects of other factors. If bilingualism has been voluntary, one would expect that parents who have positive and open attitudes themselves would be more inclined than those who do not, to, for example, place their children in a bilingual education programme at school. Inter-marriage itself shows that parents have open attitudes toward other ethnic groups and value systems. Thus, it is not necessarily bilingualism which may cause eventual positive effects but, rather, the fact that the child is exposed to certain positive attitudes from parents. Similarly, negative effects may not be due to bilingualism per se but rather to other factors such as negative attitudes of others towards one's ethnic or cultural group.

With these limitations in mind, some results will, nevertheless, be mentioned which have found bilingualism to have a positive effect on the child's social development. For example, in one study bilingual and monolingual children were given a task in which they were asked to explain a simple game to two listeners, one who was blindfolded and one who was not. The results showed that the bilingual children, more often than the monolinguals, gave information concerning the physical aspects of the game to the blindfolded listener than to the non-blindfolded one. This was interpreted as showing that bilingual children, as a result of their own communication experiences, may be more able than monolinguals to assume the roles of others experiencing communication difficulties, to perceive their needs, and to respond to these needs.

These results were supported in interviews with parents raising their children bilingually in Sweden. Several of the parents suggested that the experience of bilingualism and biculturalism had resulted in their children showing an early concern about others and a positive reaction to the peoples of other cultures.

Conclusions

Parents hoping to find some definite answers concerning the effects of bilingualism will perhaps be disappointed by the present chapter. Nevertheless, it is hoped that the discussion has given some insight into the difficulties of carrying out research in this area which in turn will allow parents to develop a more critical attitude towards information which is received in the future concerning the effects of bilingualism.

In summary, research findings at the present time have not indicated that bilingualism has either positive or negative effects on children's development. As a well-known expert in the field has suggested:

"In short, almost no general statements are warranted by research on the effects of early bilingualism. It has not been demonstrated that early bilingualism has positive or negative consequences for language development, cognitive functioning, or intellectual development. In each of these areas the findings of research are either contradicted by other research or can be questioned on methodological grounds. The one statement that is supported by research findings is that command of a second language makes a difference if the child is tested in that language – a not very surprising finding" (McLaughlin, 1984: 225).

Several points are in order, however. Firstly, research results often consist of averages over groups of individuals and tell us little about the individual child. It may be the case that bilingualism presents more of an advantage to some children or even a disadvantage to others. Secondly, it must be considered that the lack of "effects" may also be due to the fact that researchers have not yet isolated those areas of the child's development which can be expected to be influenced by bilingualism in either a positive or a negative way (or developed ways of testing these areas). At any rate, it is probably safe to say that, at the present time, parents should place greater weight on other factors than those related to the effects of bilingualism in their decisions concerning whether or not to raise their children bilingually.

4 Raising children bilingually in the family: Some research findings with regard to the minority language

Before deciding whether or not to raise one's children bilingually many parents would like to know what degree of bilingualism it is possible to achieve in their situation and how much effort will be required of them. Although definite answers are impossible to give due to the fact that individual family situations vary greatly, some general research findings concerning results which have been achieved in a number of studies will be mentioned.

Most studies looking at family bilingualism have focused on the mixed-language family rather than the non-mixed-language family. Perhaps this is because in the latter case it is the combination of the family with the outside environment which produces the bilingualism. All factors being equal, however, it is probably easier for a child, both of whose parents speak the minority language, to achieve a high degree of proficiency in this language than the child who only has one parent who does. This is due to the greater exposure which the child receives as well as the increased motivation to use the minority language when it is the only family language.

Parents interested in reading about the results from the many individual studies which have been carried out may wish to refer to McLaughlin's book (see "Suggestions for Further Reading"). Here, only general results with regard to the degree of bilingualism achieved will be discussed.

Results from earlier studies
of mixed-language families

In many cases the results from earlier studies of mixed-language families have been highly positive, i.e. the children have achieved high levels of proficiency in both their languages. For example, in a classic study by Ronjat in 1913 of a child learning German from his mother and French from his father while growing up in France, it was reported that the child learned both languages equally well. This was attributed to the fact that each parent had consistently used their own language when addressing the child. In other cases observed by Ronjat, where the parents had mixed the languages, the results had not been as favourable. In a more recent study by Virginia Volterra and Traute Taeschner (1978) of two sisters acquiring German and Italian in the home it was suggested that children raised bilingually in the home will "speak both languages fluently, i.e. with the same linguistic competence as a monolingual child". Other studies have also suggested similar findings, i.e. that the bilingual child is able to achieve monolingual norms in each language.

In other studies, however, less optimal results have been reported and there is increasing evidence that raising children bilingually is not as easy as has earlier been assumed. For example, in a study of 25 English-French-speaking families in France by Ruth Métraux it was found that of the 47 children studied, 19 had become "bilingual", i.e. they showed an ability to communicate equally well in two languages, 15 could speak one language well plus a certain amount of the second language, five could only understand the minority language, and five knew only French (three of the children had not begun speaking yet). Other studies have also shown that the majority language often dominates, especially as the child grows older.

Métraux's study was also important in pointing out the role of personality factors in becoming bilingual. The results showed that extroverted children who easily adapted to new situations had an easier time learning a second language than those who were introverted or slow in adapting to new situations.

Trilingualism in the mixed-language family

Many families are presented with a trilingual situation in the home. A number of studies have shown that it is also possible to obtain a fairly high degree of proficiency in three languages, these results, of course, varying in a similar way to those from bilingual settings. Hoffman (1985), for example, described the language development in her two children aged eight and five. The children were growing up in England in a family where the mother was a native speaker of German and the father a native speaker of Spanish. They heard the two minority languages from each of their parents, from different au-pair girls who were native speakers of either language, during trips to the minority language countries, and from relatives who came to visit. The children were exposed to English at a play-school at about the age of three. The younger child, however, was actually exposed to the three languages at a younger age due to the fact that his older sister often used English in the home. Here is a summary of the results with regard to the children's degree of bilingualism:

> "How successful has been our attempt to achieve trilingualism in our children? It is, of course, much too early to say: their trilingualism will be just what they make of it during their lives. Up to the present moment I can suggest an answer only in relative terms. We have succeeded in establishing a degree of linguistic competence in German and Spanish which is sufficient for all everyday practical purposes and which is also an adequate basis for the personal and emotional interaction between the children and the parents. As the children grow up, we hope that their linguistic proficiency will provide direct access to the respective cultures. English has become the dominant language, and the children are now fully indistinguishable from native English-speaking children. We consider this to be a desirable, and indeed essential, basis for their personal development in this country, for both psychological and educational reasons" (Hoffman, 1985: 493–494).

Results from studies of families where both parents speak the minority language

As was mentioned earlier, families in which both parents have emigrated from the same country often achieve better results with regard to maintaining the minority language in the home than the mixed-language family does. For example, in a study of different immigrant groups in Australia it was found that language shift (i.e. the use of the majority language only) in the second generation was much lower in families where both parents had the same immigrant background than it was in cases where parents (from the same immigrant backgrounds as above) had intermarried with native English speakers. Similar results were found in a study in Sweden by Sally Boyd from the University of Gothenburg who investigated the use of the minority language among second generation immigrant children (age 14–16) in families where both parents came from the same country or had intermarried with

Swedes or other immigrants having a different language background from their own. The results thus showed that the use of the minority language was much greater in the non-mixed families.

The results from Boyd's study also showed, however, that even in the non-mixed families, although the children used the minority language when addressing their parents, Swedish was mainly used when speaking with brothers and sisters or friends, including those having the same immigrant background. Thus, many of the homes were actually bilingual. It was thus questioned whether the minority language would survive in the long run. Two factors were pointed out, however, in connection with the children's tendency to use the majority language with all but their parents: 1) that the children had grown up before bilingual education in the schools had come into effect (it is felt that bilingual education may help in maintaining the use of a minority language): and 2) that because the children were teenagers, they might be especially sensitive to (Swedish) peer group pressure at the time when the study was carried out.

Even if parents in the non-mixed-language family situation are successful in maintaining the use of the minority language, it should be recognized that it is unlikely that their children will be able to achieve the same proficiency level in the language as they would have had they remained in the minority language country. This is especially true if the minority group is small and isolated. Many studies have shown the difficulty of maintaining a minority language when it is not used extensively in the wider environment, this having to do with both the reduced range of use as well as the influence from the majority language.

Results from a study of children growing up bilingually in Sweden in mixed-language families

I would like to illustrate the idea that it is more difficult than is generally assumed to raise children bilingually in the context of the mixed-language family with some results from a study which I carried out of four children growing up in English-Swedish-speaking families living in Sweden. The children were first studied during a one-year period when they were between two and three years old. Contact was maintained with the families after that time, however, and a follow-up study of the children was carried out again when they were approximately seven years old. These studies will be referred to as the "longitudinal" and "follow-up" studies in the following discussion. Although only four children were studied the results should be seen together with those from an interview study of 20 English-Swedish-speaking families in Sweden (Arnberg, 1979).

I became interested in carrying out research on these families because there seemed to be a great need for information concerning bilingual language development in the "normal" family. Many of the problems which these families seemed to be experiencing had been overlooked in the research literature, in my opinion.

The study involved three girls and a boy. Two of the children had older brothers or sisters while two were single children. All of the mothers were native English speakers who had lived in Sweden from three to six years when the study began. All of the fathers were native Swedish speakers. All of the fathers and one of the mothers had completed studies at the university level.

The main goals of the study were to look at:
1. the degree of bilingualism achieved by the children;
2. interference in each language;
3. the language pattern in the families;
4. factors explaining the results with regard to the children's degree of bilingualism.

The discussion here will focus on points (1) and (4), whereas point (2) is discussed in Chapters 3 and 6 and point (3) in Chapter 7.

During the longitudinal study the children were visited in their homes and observed while interacting with each parent. In all cases the experimenter was strictly an observer in the families in order to obtain, as much as possible, a picture of what was actually occurring in the families. The children were observed while interacting with their English-speaking mothers once a month and with their Swedish-speaking fathers approximately three times during the year.

The results showed that even at the age of two the children mainly spoke to their English-speaking mothers in Swedish. Typical in all the families was the occurrence of bilingual conversations in which the mothers addressed their children in English and were responded to in Swedish by their children. During the six-month period preceding the summer (when three of the children visited the English-speaking country) the percentage of utterances addressed to the mothers which were entirely in Swedish ranged from 76 to 91 for the different children. Even when the children spoke "English", however, this was often in the form of one-word utterances or the insertion of English words and phrases in sentences which were otherwise entirely in Swedish.

In looking at the results over the year, a slight decrease was found in the use of English for the three oldest children during the period up to the visit to the English-speaking country. The trip had an important influence on the children's use of English, however, especially for one child. In this case the child's use of English to the mother increased from 12% of the total utterances before the trip to 73% after the trip. According to the mother this dramatic improvement was in large part due to the child having participated in a summer day camp programme, following which the mother reported that the child "refused to speak Swedish" for the remainder of the stay in the English-speaking country.

These results can be compared with those from another of the children whose use of English with the mother following the trip showed only a slight increase. In this case the mother stated that the child had spoken Swedish during the entire six-week visit to the English-speaking country. Of interest were the mother's comments concerning the lack of English-speaking playmates during the visit. Thus, trips to the English-speaking country, although important, may have a greater impact if they involve the opportunity for the child to interact with other children.

With regard to the children's Swedish, however, development in this language appeared to be progressing normally. The length of the children's utterances (this being a common measure used by researchers to judge children's progress in language development) showed a similar pattern of development to that of monolingual Swedish-speaking children taking part in another research study. Nevertheless, it should be recognized that utterance length gives only a rough picture of the ability to use a language. It is thus highly important that in future studies of family bilingualism more comprehensive measures of the child's language development in the majority language be carried out.

With regard to why the children so infrequently spoke the minority language to their mothers, two factors were felt to be important; firstly, the children's lack of exposure to English (and, as a result, the greater effort required when speaking this language) and, secondly, their lack of motivation to use English. The children appeared to be unmotivated to use English for two reasons: 1) because they could already communicate adequately in another language and, 2) because they were understood by and responded to by their English-speaking mothers even when Swedish was used. The importance of the children's motivation can be illustrated by the dramatic improvement in English when playing with other children during the visit to the English-speaking country. The children's willingness to use English when they were motivated to do so was also shown by one of the children who, during the last observation session, translated (into English) everything she had just said (in Swedish) to her English-speaking mother for the experimenter so that she would "understand".

Thus, in conclusion, this study showed the difficulty of developing a high degree of proficiency in the minority language in the situation where input in this language was mainly restricted to only one adult in the child's environment. It should be mentioned, however, that some parents do manage to raise their children bilingually even in such seemingly adverse circumstances. We will look at some of the factors which seem to be involved in successfully raising a child bilingually at the end of this chapter.

Follow-up of the children at the age of seven

Continued contact with these bilingual families over the years has been invaluable in terms of learning more about children's bilingual language development as well as family bilingualism, e.g. how patterns of using the language in the family are influenced by outside factors such as the children starting school, the birth of younger brothers and sisters, parents returning to work, etc. At the age of seven a sample of the children's speech was taped again while interacting with each parent using the same method as that used earlier.

At this time, Swedish was felt to be the dominant language for all of the children. This result seems inevitable considering the fact that the parents estimated the children's daily exposure to Swedish, as opposed to English, to vary from between 65 to 90% for the different children. The children's dominance in Swedish was also demonstrated in a simple word-naming task in which the children were asked to name as many things as they could think of related to the areas of home, school, and neighbourhood in one minute, according to a method used by Saunders (1982). The task is carried out in both languages and the results are given on a scale from 0 to 1 with 0.50 indicating "balance" and 1 indicating, in the present case, that all responses were in Swedish. The results for the four children agree with parents' judgements of their children's bilingualism, showing a clear dominance in Swedish in all areas (see Table 1).

The children's language development in Swedish appeared to be progressing normally according to the results from a receptive vocabulary test (in such tests children only need to point to the correct form rather than saying it themselves) in which the children were compared with monolingual Swedish-speaking children. This was also supported by several of the children's teachers who, according to parents, had commented on the unusually large Swedish vocabularies of the children.

In the English version of the vocabulary test, however, the children performed at several years below norms for their age levels (see Figure 1).

Figure 1 also shows the irregular pattern of the children's language development in the minority language in comparison with children having this language as their native tongue (the latter shown by the solid line).

TABLE 1   *Degree of bilingualism for four bilingual children in three domains*

Domain	Score			
	T	*L*	*S*	*F*
Home	0.68	0.71	0.92	0.76
School	0.77	0.57	1.00	0.74
Neighbourhood	0.86	0.70	0.93	0.70
Mean	0.77	0.66	0.95	0.73

In order to obtain a general picture of the children's use of English and Swedish, fluency and accuracy in both languages were measured for the first 50 utterances in the speech samples taken while they were interacting with each parent. The utterances in each language were measured for the following: the average number of words per utterance; the number of errors made per 100 words; the number of words produced per minute; the total number of words produced in the 50 utterances; and the time required to produce 50 utterances. Table 2 shows the children's greater fluency and accuracy when speaking Swedish than when speaking English.

The sample of 50 utterances was also examined for the types of mistakes the children made in each language. Few mistakes were made in Swedish, but many were made in English. Space does not permit a detailed description of the children's errors; however, in general they were related to the following areas: word order, verb forms, pluralization forms, use of articles, semantic interference (i.e. the transfer of the meaning of a word from the other language), lexical interference (i.e. the transfer of a word from the other language), and phonological interference (i.e. the transfer of sound patterns from the other language). Parents will perhaps recall from the last chapter, however, that not all of the language errors of the bilingual child can be attributed to interference from the other language; many instead may be similar to normal "developmental" errors made by monolingual children learning the language as their first language.

Despite the fact that all of the parents were somewhat disappointed by the results achieved with regard to the children's fluency in English, all were

positive about the effects they felt bilingualism and biculturalism seemed to
have had on their children's lives, including the following: the child's sense of
pride in his/her bilingualism and being able to manage conversations in the
English-speaking country; a wider access to ideas and experiences than that of
the monolingual child; the enriching experience of being exposed to two
cultures, and positive social benefits including a concern about others and a
positive reaction to the peoples of other cultures. The results from interviews
with the children also showed that all were positive towards their bilingualism
and felt that it was a useful thing to know two languages.

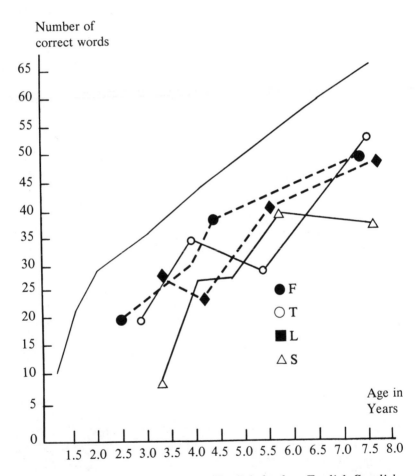

FIGURE 1 *Receptive vocabulary in English for four English-Swedish-
speaking bilingual children in comparison with mental age
norms*

In summary, the results at the age of seven showed a clear dominance in Swedish and a normal language development in that language. The children were several years below norms for their age levels in English. Nevertheless, they were able to carry out conversations in English when they were motivated to do so. These results were felt to be encouraging in light of the fact that at approximately three years old, all of the children except one, who had recently returned from a visit to the English-speaking country, were predominantly Swedish-speaking, even when speaking with their English-speaking parents.

TABLE 2 *Fluency and accuracy in English and Swedish*

Child		MLU in words	Errors per 100 words	WPM	Length in words	Time (in minutes)
L	E	4.3	9.3	21.5	215	10
	S	6.3	1.0	41.7	313	7.5
F	E	3.6	7.7	32.9	181	5.5
	S	4.8	1.7	55.8	240	4.3
T	E	3.4	12.3	24.3	170	7.0
	S	4.9	0	45.8	243	5.3
S	E	3.0	11.3	13.4	151	11.3
	S	6.1	0	70.5	303	4.3

The importance of support to parents raising their children bilingually

In my opinion, the results from the study also showed the importance of information and support to parents raising their children bilingually, which was provided indirectly through parents' participation in the study. Although one cannot, of course, over-estimate the effects of participation in a research study, the monthly interest of an outsider in the family's progress together with several spin-off effects from the study (to be discussed shortly) were, nevertheless, felt to have had an encouraging influence on several of the parents who, otherwise, may not have been motivated to continue their efforts in raising their children bilingually. It is naturally the case that some parents may be in greater need of support than others. Some parents are highly motivated to raise their children bilingually and manage to do so even in circumstances which are less than optimal. For other parents, however, information at the right time seems to be highly important.

The above-mentioned spin-off effects consisted of two activities. The first of these was the starting of a women's group in which the mothers met in each other's homes once a month. As was mentioned in Chapter 1, it is important that parents have the opportunity to discuss problems in connection with raising their children bilingually and to "compare notes". Getting together with others from the same immigrant background also allows one to identify with one's own ethnic group which is helpful in increasing motivation to raise one's child bilingually. The second spin-off effect was the starting of a minority language playgroup for the children which met once a week. The results from this group will be discussed in Chapter 10.

Nevertheless, the fact remains that the children's English was rather weak at the age of seven. To what extent further contact with the English language through speaking it, reading, trips to the English-speaking country and minority language instruction at school (in Sweden all children have the right to receive several lessons in the minority language per week) will eventually enable the children to achieve greater fluency and accuracy remains to be seen. At any rate, both parents and children have felt that bilingualism has made a positive contribution to the children's lives.

Explaining differences in research findings

Why is it the case that some research findings show that it is possible to achieve a high degree of fluency in two languages when being raised bilingually in the family, while others have not? I would like to point out several reasons making it difficult to generalize findings from some of the research literature reporting highly positive findings to the "normal" family.

Firstly, many of the parents achieving highly positive results spent a great deal of time in training their children in the minority language or went to great pains in order to increase exposure to this language. For example, in one case the parents reported not having bought a television set in order to balance the dominating influence of the majority language in the home. In another case the child was only allowed to play with other children speaking the minority language during the first two years. Furthermore, the child's grandmother was requested not to speak to him in her native language during this time in order to follow the family's strategy of only introducing one language at a time. Although such practices are well-meaning and may even be effective, they simply do not represent the actions of most parents. In fact, a reason frequently given by parents for raising their children bilingually is so that the child will be able to speak with playmates speaking the majority language as well as grandparents.

Other factors related to the background of some of the parents may also make them a special group in certain ways, e.g. the fact that many were linguists or other academics having a particular interest in language. Parents who are linguists have a professional interest in language. Not only can they be expected to be knowledgeable concerning how languages are structured and learned, but they are also highly motivated to learn and maintain languages themselves. For example, in several of the research studies, highly language-interested parents have attempted to teach their children a second language in the home when this language was not even a native language of the parent. Again, although such studies are highly interesting in that they show what *can* be accomplished in the context of the home, the results simply cannot be generalized to most families. Parents who are linguists are also likely to have friends and colleagues with an appreciation for language learning and bilingualism. Through this the parents are likely to receive support for their endeavours in raising their children bilingually. Their children are also likely to encounter positive attitudes toward becoming bilingual. Finally, it is a well-known fact that children vary greatly with regard to skills, interests, etc. Some children are more artistic, musical, athletic, or technically interested than others. Thus, it may be the case that some children are more interested in and skilled at learning languages than others and that a genetic factor may even have been involved in cases where the parents were linguists.

These results are, of course, in no way intended to discourage parents from raising their children bilingually but rather to help them in forming realistic expectations as well as recognizing the importance of a number of factors if they are to successfully raise their children bilingually. These include the following:

- maintaining a positive attitude toward bilingualism;
- making a conscious decision to raise one's child bilingually and following through with this;
- giving language learning priority;
- ensuring that the child receives as much exposure as possible to both languages.

Does one need to be an "expert" then, to successfully raise a child bilingually? I believe that the answer to this question is "No", although it must also be recognized that bilingualism is a matter of degree. Moreover, researchers have learned more and more about the process of learning two (or more) languages which can be of help to all parents in raising their children bilingually. In the remaining chapters we will look at some of these research findings as well as some practical suggestions focusing on how to go about raising one's child bilingually.

PART III:
How should I raise
my child bilingually?

Having now made the decision to raise one's child bilingually, a number of other decisions still remain for parents. These include questions such as how the two languages should be used in the home, when the second language (i.e. the majority language) should be introduced, in which language the child should be educated, etc. Part III focuses on these issues. In Chapter 5 a general introduction is given concerning how children learn language. This background is felt to be important for parents raising their children bilingually, regardless of which approach is taken. Chapter 6 looks more closely at language learning in the bilingual child, including a discussion of different ways of presenting the two languages, i.e. simultaneous and successive bilingualism. In Chapter 7 strategies for using the two languages in the bilingual family are focused on. Finally, in Chapter 8 different goals which families can aim toward with regard to raising their children bilingually are discussed.

5 How children learn language

A basic understanding of how children learn language is important for parents raising their children bilingually so that they can understand their own role in this process. Although the bilingual child is in the process of learning two languages, in its general nature, the learning process is similar to that of the monolingual child (or to that of the multilingual child for that matter).

In any scientific field the goal of research is not only to *describe* a given phenomenon but also to try and *explain* it. In this way one can begin to make sense of the various pieces of information available. This situation is no different in the field of children's language development where researchers have also tried to give explanations for how this process takes place. Although our understanding of the area is still far from complete, enormous progress has been made in the past 25 years or so and the present chapter will describe the major explanations which have appeared in the field.

Although researchers in the past have tended to accept one explanation to the exclusion of others, a more recent approach has been to accept the role of several different explanations, as no one explanation on its own has been shown to give a completely satisfactory account of the developmental process. Such an approach is suggested by the British child-language researcher, Gordon Wells, and will be the approach taken in this chapter. Wells suggests the following:

"Proponents of the different theories tend to present them as if they were in competition, but it is probably better to see them as each contributing cumulatively to an increasingly rounded account. Certainly it is our view that, with each new emphasis, the account that can be given of development has been progressively enriched" (1981: 74).

Another theme in the research attempting to explain how the child learns language, concerns the emphasis which researchers have placed on the role of: 1) the environment and, 2) inborn abilities within the child. Although

47

researchers may not agree concerning which of these factors is *most* important, it is probably fair to say that most experts in the field see language development in terms of a complex interaction between environmental factors and inborn abilities.

In the following discussion, parents' understanding of the developments in the field will be enhanced if the two above factors are kept in mind, i.e.:

1. the need for a combination of explanations in accounting for how language development takes place;
2. the differences in emphasis which various researchers have placed on environmental factors and inborn abilities.

It may also be helpful if parents attempt to visualize the developments in terms of a "spiral" revolving alternately between "environmental" and "inborn" explanations. At the same time, the spiral moves upward, increasing in volume as new explanations are added and knowledge is increased.

In the following discussion five explanations for how language development takes place will be presented. The order in which they are presented should not be seen as indicating their relative importance, however. These are:

– outer reinforcement;
– certain pre-programmed abilities;
– an active drive to structure the world, including language;
– active interaction with care-givers and others;
– imitation and modelling with and without complete understanding of that which has been imitated/modelled.

Explanations emphasizing the role of outer reinforcement

The first formal theory for how the child develops language considered the environment to be the most important factor. Researchers taking this viewpoint felt that the child could be taught anything if fed with information in the right way. The child, according to this theory, was seen as a *tabula rasa* (Latin for "scraped tablet") to be filled with knowledge.

According to this theory, language learning occurs because of rewards (or reinforcement). The child is positively reinforced, mainly by parents or other care-givers, for producing correct sounds, words, phrases, or sentences while incorrect forms are negatively reinforced. Often this reinforcement is given unconsciously by parents.

In the beginning, adults may positively reinforce the child for any type of verbalization which is produced, but eventually more and more is demanded of the child, i.e. the adult requires that a correct response is given before approval is shown. In this way the child's behaviour is shaped. For example, the child may first use the word "dog" to refer to all small animals having four legs and a tail, cats included! The adult, by gradually reinforcing the child only when the word is used in the correct situation, helps the child to learn the meaning of the word "dog".

Although reinforcement certainly seems to play a role in some aspects of the child's language learning, as a general explanation for how language learning takes place it has not been found to be very adequate. This has led to the development of other theories to explain the language learning process.

The child as "pre-programmed" to learn language

The strongest reaction against explanations based on outer reinforcement came from the American linguist, Noam Chomsky, who felt that explanations based on processes such as reinforcement could not account for many aspects of language development. These include the highly creative nature of language development or the speed with which it occurs. Instead of language learning occurring because of factors in the outside environment, it was suggested that children are born with the ability to learn language. Other arguments for an inborn ability are that children all over the world learn language at approximately the same age and seem to learn it in a similar manner.

According to Chomsky and others, there are universal (i.e. the same for all children regardless of language) principles built into the brain which allow the child to analyse the language it hears and to sort out the bits and pieces of information into a formal system of rules for understanding and producing language. By "rules" one does not mean the type of rules found in a grammar book but, rather, the ability which most adults have to speak in well-formed utterances which can be understood by others speaking in the same language. Chomsky referred to this ability as the LAD (Language Acquisition Device). (Of course this is not a real organ in the brain but just an analogy.) The following diagram is a suggestion of how the LAD works.

Theories suggesting that the child is pre-programmed to learn language thus suggest that the basic principles for forming grammar exist in the brain, waiting to "unfold" as the child matures. Although the child must, of course, be exposed to language in order for it to develop, the role of adults and of the environment is seen as mainly activating that which is already present in the child.

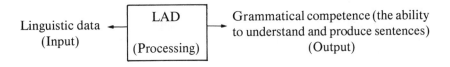

Chomsky's ideas had an enormous influence on researchers investigating children's language development in the 1960's. Many studies were carried out investigating what rules children use in producing and understanding language at various stages of their development. Nevertheless, the theory began to receive increasing criticism as, according to many researchers, it is far too limited. Language learning is felt to involve much more than the acquisition of a system of grammatical rules for generating sentences. Such an explanation does not consider the fact that, at least in the beginning, language is used to label concepts which the child has already acquired *non-verbally* through interaction with objects in the environment. In other words, Chomsky's theory does not seem to emphasize the role of the child's cognitive development in language learning to a great enough extent. Furthermore, language learning does not occur in a social vacuum as Chomsky seemed to suggest. Instead, from the beginning, it is experienced as a means of communication with significant others (Snow & Ferguson, 1977).

In relation to the last point, one reason for proposing an innate ability was that it was assumed that the speech which children heard around them was so "fragmented and confusing" that they must surely have to rely on inborn capacities. Research findings concerning the speech which parents use when addressing their children, however, has not supported this idea. On the contrary, it has been found that parents' speech to children seems ideally suited in helping them to learn language. For example, adults have been found to adapt their speech to children, speaking to young children in a different way than they do, say, to adults or older children. Typical "techniques" of parents include the use of short, simple sentences, lots of repetition, attention-getters such as using the child's name, a rising intonation at the end of sentences, etc.

These research findings regarding the help from the environment which the child receives, cast doubt on the idea that an innate LAD can be entirely responsible for the child's language learning. This does not, of course, deny the role of biological factors in language development. Nevertheless, other factors, aside from purely biological ones, are seen as also playing an important role in the child's language development.

Explanations emphasizing
the active role of the child

In both the "outer reinforcement" and the "pre-programmed" explanations, the child is given a rather passive role in which language learning is seen as occurring, either because of an influence from the environment, or an activation of innate abilities. With reference to the latter point, researchers supporting the Chomskyian position have suggested, for example, that learning to talk is similar to the maturation of a physical process like learning to walk. Thus, it is suggested that children "cannot help learning to talk".

The next stage in the spiral highlights, instead, the active role played by the child, both in terms of an inner motivation which results from a need to explain and understand the world, and in a social need to communicate and interact with others which starts from the first moment of birth. This explanation does not deny the role of earlier mentioned factors such as reinforcement or innate abilities. The child, nevertheless, according to this theory is seen as a highly active "person" having a strong inner drive to learn to understand, handle, and control the environment in which it exists. According to the Swiss developmental psychologist, Jean Piaget, the child does this by adapting information from the world to existing mental structures (or ideas about the world). These structures are then gradually reorganized as new information "fails to fit" with existing structures and as better ways of understanding the world are perceived by the child. The child does not need to be influenced by anyone to carry out this task; it is an inborn need which is shared with all higher animals and which is essential for survival. Language learning, according to this theory, is thus seen as being acquired in a similar way to other types of knowledge.

Finally, as the spiral turns again, there are explanations which, although they continue to emphasize the role of the child as an active seeker of meaningfulness in its environment, emphasize the role of the environment to a greater extent. Such explanations see language as developing in a context of interaction and communication with others who are highly important in the child's life and where the meaning and purpose exchanged during conversations is as important as the actual sounds, words, and phrases which the child learns to produce.

Wells (1981) explains how language learning is experienced as communication from the very beginning. By treating the baby's contributions (i.e. various gurgles, burps, and coos) as conversational turns during the routines of washing, feeding, diapering, dressing, etc. the child learns to participate in conversations before it actually begins to talk. Through frequent repetition of words and phrases by parents during these routines the child gradually learns to match the form of what the mother is saying with the actual activity being carried out. In continued conversations with adults and others in which the child plays an increasingly active role, the child, through listening and speaking about a commonly focused-on topic, learns to exchange meaning and to elaborate and expand on these meanings. Thus, from the very beginning, language is experienced by the child as *communication*.

Explanations emphasizing
the role of imitation and modelling

Finally, parallel with the above developments, a number of experiments and observations have made it clear that imitation and modelling also play an important role in learning. Researchers such as Albert Bandura suggest that much of what the child learns results from observations and imitation of others, in most cases without reinforcement occurring at all.

With regard to language learning, although researchers such as Chomsky have tended to debunk the role of processes such as imitation in language acquisition, as has been mentioned earlier, children cannot acquire vocabulary and grammar without exposure to models. Children hear language all around them and even if they do not imitate directly, they are continually taking in information about the language they hear which may be reactivated at a later stage through the process of delayed imitation. Thus, it is unlikely that imitation and modelling do not play some role in the child's language development. There is evidence that, at least in some cultures, imitation may play a highly important role in the child's language learning. For example, Ochs and Schieffelin (1984) report that the Kaluli of Papua New Guinea use imitation as a direct teaching strategy in showing their children how to speak by first providing a model utterance followed by an imperative meaning "Say like that".

In imitation the child may pick up smaller or larger "chunks" of language which they use before really understanding the meaning of the individual words or other units. Some striking evidence for this is provided from studies of children acquiring a second language at an early age. For example, in a study by Joseph Huang and Evelyn Hatch (1978), a young Chinese boy, Paul, was observed during his first encounter with English at a play-school. The researchers found much evidence of Paul's use of imitation in the first stages of acquiring English. Only three weeks after Paul had entered the play-school he had learned certain words, phrases, and greetings through imitation, e.g.:

Get out of here;
Let's go;

Don't do that;
It's time to eat and drink.

Such utterances were often learned in connection with routines which were repeated every day, such as that in the last example, said each day before snack time. Yet, as the researchers pointed out, these phrases were learned as unanalysed units. For example, Paul could not break them up or recombine them with other words (i.e. he never said "It's time to . . ." in connection with anything else). As time progressed, however, Paul began to produce a different type of utterance which showed evidence of his own creative construction of language and which was not the result of direct imitation.

Evidence of imitation can also be found in children acquiring their first language. Early imitation has sometimes been called "imitation with reduction" because the young child, rather than reproducing the adult's utterance word for word, reduces it "to its bare essentials". For example, in imitation of the sentence, "It's not the same dog as Pepper", the child was heard to reply, "Dog, Pepper" (Brown, 1965). One explanation for this is the limited memory capacity of the young child, although other explanations have also been suggested.

Summary

Five factors have been discussed which play a role in the child's language development. These are:

- outer reinforcement;
- certain pre-programmed structures;
- an active drive to structure the world, including language;
- active interaction with care-givers and others;
- imitation and modelling with and without complete understanding of what is imitated/modelled.

Even if a theory of language development considers all of the above factors to be important, it remains unclear as to what the role of each factor is or how the various factors interact with one another. Some factors, such as interaction with care-givers and the child's drive to structure the world, certainly seem to play a more important role in language development than others, such as imitation and reinforcement. Nevertheless, an answer to the above question will undoubtedly require many years of research. At any rate, the relevance of the above factors for parents raising their children bilingually will be discussed in the final section of the chapter.

Landmarks in children's language development

In addition to understanding *how* the child develops language, a general understanding of the developmental process itself, i.e. *what* skills children develop at different ages, is also important. Although research findings have given a good picture of the normal pattern of development, parents should nevertheless realize that children vary greatly with regard to the speed at which they learn language. As has been pointed out earlier, this does not seem to be a result of bilingualism but, rather, is a characteristic of normal development.

In learning any language the child faces a number of highly complex tasks, including the following: (Reference to the branches of linguistics which deal specifically with these areas is given in parentheses).

-   learning the sound system of the language (phonology);
-   learning how to form words and to combine these into increasingly complex utterances (syntax);
-   learning the meaning of words as well as how words are combined to form meanings in sentences (semantics);
-   learning how to use language in order to communicate with others (communication).

Development of the sound system

Early development

There are a number of indications that human infants are "biologically prepared" for the development of speech. For example, at 24 hours after birth, infants are already able to synchronize their own movements (of the head, arms, legs, etc.) with the speech they hear around them. Furthermore, they react to the human voice rather than to other noises such as rhythmical beating (Condon & Sander, 1974). Infants who are only one month old are already able to distinguish certain speech sounds from one another such as "ba" and "pa" (Eimas *et al.*, 1971).

During recent years researchers have become increasingly interested in the infant's verbal behaviour during the first year of life and the relation of this to later language development. Researchers such as Stark (1980) and Oller (1980), by studying a number of infants, have identified various stages of development which the infant passes through. (These stages are felt to be similar for all infants regardless of what language is spoken around them.) Stark (1980), for example, suggests that development proceeds in the following general way. (Individual variation may also occur, however.)

Up to about six weeks of age the vocal noises which the baby produces consist of forms of crying and other sounds such as sputtering and burping. Cooing and laughter appear at 6–16 weeks. During the third stage occurring at 16–30 weeks the baby's sound production consists of vocal play involving sounds such as squealing, yelling, and the noises produced by blowing air or food through constrictions of the mouth, etc. Researchers refer to the fourth stage, occurring at 6–10 months, as "reduplicated babbling". Babbling during this stage consists of consonant-vowel sequences which are repeated (e.g. "baba", "dada", etc.). Stage five at 10–14 months has been referred to as non-reduplicated babbling. During this stage more varied sound combinations appear. In addition to the consonant-vowel combinations produced earlier, forms may consist, for example, of vowels alone, vowel-consonant sequences, or consonant-vowel-consonant sequences. Furthermore, different vowels and consonants are combined with each other (in contrast to the earlier repetition of the same sounds). The baby's sound production also begins to take on a much more varied stress and intonation pattern than earlier. Stage six, usually beginning when the baby is 10–12 months, consists of the production of single words. It is often difficult to agree on exactly when the first words appear because the child's pronunciation of a word often differs markedly from that of the adult's. "Words" in this sense thus usually means the child's consistent use of a certain sound pattern to refer to a particular phenomenon.

As the baby begins with the babbling stage the range of speech sounds (i.e. vowels and consonants) greatly increases due to the maturation of the speech organs. At first the babbling of all babies seems to be similar, but gradually the infant begins to be influenced by the specific language it is exposed to in its environment. It is not clear, however, exactly when this occurs. Another interesting question, about which rather little is known, concerns the babbling of bilingual infants. For example, do such infants have a larger repertoire of speech sounds than do monolingual infants, due to the exposure to two languages in their environment?

Although it was earlier believed that the child's babbling and the production of early words were entirely separate processes, most researchers now have a different viewpoint. For example, Oller (1975) and Vihman *et al.* (1985; in press) have shown that there is a striking correspondence between the sounds produced during late babbling and those appearing in the child's first words, thus linking the two processes. Furthermore, even when the first words appear, many children continue to babble, e.g. when they are playing by themselves.

Later development

It is not until the child has mastered approximately 25–50 words that one can really talk about the development of the sound system in any reliable way

(Linell & Jennische, 1980). Before this period the speech material available for analysis is much too limited. The most well-known theory for how the sound system develops is that of Roman Jakobson (1941). Essentially this theory predicts the order in which certain sound contrasts in the language will develop.

In every human language there are a small number of contrasts in the way that the sounds of the language are produced. Some of these contrasts are gross while others are much more subtle. In very simple terms, Jakobson's theory suggests that the grosser the contrast is between two sounds, the more easily it will be perceived and produced by the child. (And, consequently, the earlier it will appear in the child's speech.) In other words, the child begins with the gross contrasts gradually adding finer and finer distinctions as the system develops.

The first contrast to appear is that between vowel and consonant. The vowel and consonant which contrast the most with each other (in terms of how they are produced) are "a" and "p" or "b". (The only difference between "p" and "b" is that the first sound is produced when the vocal cords are apart and the other when they are vibrating.) The next contrast to appear is that between oral and nasal consonants. (Oral consonants are produced when the airstream from the lungs is stopped in the mouth while in nasal consonants the air escapes through the nose.) At this time the baby is able to produce sounds such as "ba", "pa", "baba", "papa", and "mama". The next contrast to appear is between consonants made with the lips (bilabials) and those made when the tip or blade of the tongue is placed against the upper front teeth (dentals). This distinction is applied for each of the oral and nasal sounds acquired earlier. The following diagram (from Clark & Clark, 1977) may help to illustrate the above process more clearly.

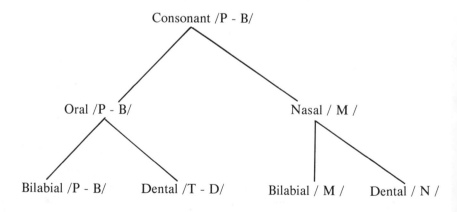

The sound system continues to develop in this way. The theory not only predicts the order in which sounds will develop but also explains the child's sound substitutions. Sounds representing more subtle contrasts are replaced by those having more pronounced contrasts, e.g. the child's pronunciation of the word "suit" as "tut".

Although in general Jakobson's predictions have been supported, the theory has also received some criticism. First of all, learning sound contrasts does not seem to be the way in which children go about learning the sounds of the language they are exposed to. Instead, their goal seems to be to try to pronounce the words and phrases they hear spoken around them as best they can. Some evidence of a "word" strategy is that when contrasts are learned, they are not automatically applied to other situations in which they are required. This would be expected if children were using a "contrast" strategy. Furthermore, there are rather substantial differences among children in the order in which the various sounds appear. This also tends to weaken the theory.

In addition to the sounds of the language being acquired in a certain order, another characteristic of children's speech is that it is a simplified version of adult speech. Smith (1973) suggests that children simplify their speech in the following ways:

- they omit final sounds, e.g. leaving out the "t" in "boot". (This usually disappears by about the age of three);
- they reduce combinations of consonants, e.g. pronouncing "stop" as "top" or "bring" as "bing";
- they omit unstressed syllables, e.g. pronouncing the word "away" as "way";
- they reduplicate one of the syllables in a word having different syllables, e.g. pronouncing the word "daddy" as "dada".

As is the case with the disappearance of the omission of final sounds, the above simplifications gradually disappear as the child's language development progresses. Clark and Clark (1977) have suggested several reasons why the child simplifies its language. The idea which has received the most support is that children do this because they have only a limited ability to articulate sounds during the early stages of language development. As is the case with learning any skill, it may take months of practice before the skill is perfected. Some support for this explanation is that children are able to distinguish sounds when they listen to language, although they cannot yet produce the same sounds themselves. For example, children do not accept adults imitating the child's incorrect form, insisting upon the correct one. If other explanations for simplifications were true, e.g. a limited memory span so that only a portion of the adult form was held in memory, the above difference between comprehension and production would be difficult to explain.

The age at which the sound system is mastered varies according to the language being learned, this usually occurring between five and eight years of age.

First words and word combinations

Enormous progress can be seen during the pre-school years with regard to the child's development of the grammatical system of the language. From the appearance of two-word utterances at approximately two years of age, the child goes on to produce highly complex utterances by the age of four. The first words usually appear at about 12 months of age. A typical characteristic of the child's use of single words is that they are used to express a variety of intentions. For example, the child's use of the word "car" could mean, among other things:

That is a car;
Give me the car;
I am moving the car;
The car is broken (said while crying).

Because of the many possible interpretations of the child's one-word utterances, speech during this period is highly bound to the context in which it occurs, in order for the child's intentions to be correctly interpreted.

At approximately 18–24 months children begin to combine words, beginning with two-word utterances such as the following:

See doggie;
Allgone cookie;
More drink;
Throw ball.

These utterances are sometimes called "telegraphic" because they include words carrying a lot of meaning such as nouns, verbs, and adjectives while eliminating "less important" words such as prepositions, conjunctions, articles and various inflections.

Sometime before children go on to produce three-word utterances, certain intermediate forms may appear such as the utterances "Daddy read" and "Read book" following in quick succession. However, the child is not yet able to produce the utterance "Daddy read book" although such utterances are not far behind. By the time three-word utterances appear, the child's language development begins to make rapid strides. As sentences increase in complexity, the "smaller" words such as prepositions, inflections for the past tense and plural forms, articles, etc. which were omitted earlier, begin to appear. As the child's language progresses, it begins to resemble the adult's utterances more and more. Nevertheless, it is not until about the age of 12 (this probably differing somewhat for different languages) that the child has learned all of the syntactic patterns used in the language. Much more complex forms (e.g. compound sentences and different types of subordinate clauses) take many years to develop.

Individual differences

The above description of the child's language development, i.e. starting with single words and gradually building longer and more complex utterances, has been the pattern most frequently described by researchers. In a study by Ann Peters in 1977, however, attention was brought to the fact that there may be important individual differences in the way in which children develop language. In Peters' study of a little boy named Minh (from about seven months to two years of age) she found that the child was actually producing two types of speech which were used in different social situations. One type of speech was similar to the developmental pattern described above (i.e. "starting with the parts and building up the whole"). This Peters referred to as an *analytic* style. In the other speech style, Minh produced long sequences of speech. Although these strongly resembled adult speech in their intonation pattern, the individual words used were often difficult for the researcher to understand. In other words, in this second speech style, Minh seemed to be aiming towards producing whole sentences. Peters thus suggested that language development for some children may progress "from the whole to the various parts", an approach which she called a *gestalt* style. Language in a gestalt approach crystallizes out of the child's attempt to produce whole sentences rather than building up one unit at a time, i.e. progressing from the one-word stage to the two-word stage, etc. (The reader may recognize certain parallels between this discussion and the discussion of the role of imitation in second language learning appearing earlier in the chapter.)

In looking at the findings from other research studies, Peters found support for her idea that children may approach the task of learning language in different ways. In accordance with this idea, she suggested that there may be three types of language learners:

1. those who use an analytic approach from the beginning;
2. those who use both an analytic and gestalt approach (like Minh);
3. those who begin with a gestalt approach and then switch to an analytic approach.

In conclusion, parents may thus want to be aware of the fact that there are different ways in which their children may learn language. How these different learning styles are reflected in the child learning two (or more) languages has to my knowledge not yet been investigated.

Learning the meaning of words

In addition to learning the sounds and grammatical patterns of the language, the child must also learn the meaning of words, i.e. how words are used to represent external objects, events, activities, etc. in the child's life. It should be pointed out that this is only one aspect of the development of the semantic (or meaning) system of the language. For example, children's early sentences also represent underlying semantic relationships. Bloom (1970) was one of the first researchers to point this out showing how the utterance "Mommy sock" was used on two separate occasions to refer to: 1) a child picking up her mother's sock and, 2) the mother putting the child's sock on her. However, we will limit our discussion here to the learning of the meaning of words, concentrating mainly on the learning of the meaning of words for objects.

The child's vocabulary expands rapidly during the pre-school years. By the age of two most children have a vocabulary of about 300 words which they can use or understand, by the age of three this increases to about 1000 words, and between the ages of three and five over 50 words are added each month. The earliest words are often nouns related to objects, events, relationships, etc. which are important in the child's life. Thus, words for family members, foods, and animals are among those frequently reported as appearing earliest. The child's attention seems to be particularly captured by things that move. On the other hand, some researchers suggest that the earliest words may represent interpersonal functions such as greeting, requesting something from another person, or regulating another person's behaviour.

One reason for differences in reports concerning the kinds of words which are learned first may, again, be attributed to individual differences among individual children. This was pointed out by Katherine Nelson (1973) who studied the early vocabulary development in 18 children. Nelson noticed two types of learners among her subjects. At one extreme were children whom she called "referential" learners. At the other were children whom she called "expressive" learners. The referential children were found mainly to have the names of objects in their early vocabulary while the expressive children's vocabulary mainly contained words related to social activities, e.g. "bye", "naughty", etc. Thus, it seemed that language served different functions for different children. These styles were also somewhat related to the ways in which the child's mother used language when interacting with him/her.

It is important to realize that one way of learning language should not be seen as being superior to the other. Neither group showed a difference in the length of their utterances or in other measures of grammatical development. Rather, the children seemed to have different concerns in connection with language, one group being focused on objects and their characteristics while the other group seemed to be focused on people and social relationships. As was also pointed out by Nelson, many children, of course, fall in between these two extreme groups.

Another important factor to consider in early word learning is the importance of emotions, i.e. that children probably first learn words which are emotionally significant to them. This was demonstrated in a study by Whitehurst and his colleagues (1982). In this study children were shown different toys and a note was made concerning the toy which they liked best. Afterwards, the children were taught novel names for these toys. It was found that the children most easily learned the names for the toys which they liked the best.

De Villiers and de Villiers (1978) point out that the words children learn vary greatly in complexity with regard to their meaning. Among the simplest words for the child to learn are those involving proper names such as "John" or "Fido" because these refer to only one particular example. Common names such as "dog", "chair", etc. are more difficult because they involve groups of objects which are related to each other in a complex way. Relational words such as big/little or tall/short are even more difficult because they involve having to change a standard in connection with the object being described (e.g. one cannot use the same standard when talking about a big mosquito and a big elephant) as well as in connection with the context in which it occurs. Relational terms, such as "this", "that", "here", and "there", are especially difficult as they require both complex standards of comparison as well as shifts in viewpoint between speaker and listener.

With regard to the development of the meaning of words for objects, typical behaviours are that children often over- and under-extend the meanings of words. Over-extension means that the child gives a wider range of use to the word than the adult does. For example, the child might use the word "doggie" to refer to all four-legged animals. The child may also under-extend the meaning of words, i.e. use the word in a more narrow sense than the adult does. Bloom (1973) described one child's use of the word "car" only in connection with cars moving on the street outside. In other words, the child did not use the word "car" to refer to other examples of cars such as pictures of cars in books, cars which were not moving, or cars which the child rode in.

Barrett (1982) gives an explanation for the child's over- and under-extensions in his theory about how children learn the meaning of object names in general. He suggests that the child first learns the meaning of the word in terms of a "prototype referent". This simply means that the child learns the meaning of the word in reference to one particular example (or several highly similar examples) appearing frequently in the child's environment. Thus, the above "car" example may have occurred because the child was mainly exposed to the word "car" in connection with looking at moving cars outside the window.

During the next stage the child identifies certain central characteristics of the particular example (e.g. "four legged" in connection with "dog"). Having identified these the child assigns the "word" to a category of other "words" sharing similar features. It is only during this stage that over-extensions can occur. That is, when a category such as "four-legged" has not been "filled up" with other items such as cats, horses, and lions, the child will use the one word it possesses, i.e. "doggie" to refer to these other examples. As the category fills up with more and more items, the child begins to contrast the features of these with one another so that gradually items are distinguished and over-extensions disappear.

It should also be understood, of course, that the child's learning of the meaning of words has much to do with its non-linguistic experiences, i.e. the child's "knowledge about the world". Long before the child has learned the word "pillow", for example, he will probably have touched, smelled, or even tasted a pillow, this giving him certain clues about the meaning of the word as well as experiences in connection with it. Thus, there is most likely an interaction between the child's non-verbal experiences in the world and the labelling of these experiences by adults or older children in the child's learning of the meaning of certain words.

Although the role of the child's own experiences is thus important, parents should, nevertheless, realize the important role they themselves play in facilitating the learning of word meaning. This occurs, for example, in connection with naming objects during daily routines such as feeding, bathing, etc. Most parents also participate in "naming games" with their young children. It is generally felt that such activities, by allowing the child to focus on a particular phenomenon while at the same time hearing this referred to by a particular label, greatly enhance the learning of word meaning.

The present discussion has only focused on a limited area of the child's learning of meaning, i.e. on how the meaning of names for objects develops. As was the case with the development of more complex grammatical patterns throughout childhood, the development of the child's understanding of the meaning of words also continues with age. Not only are new words added to the vocabulary, but the meaning of existing words is further elaborated and refined. As de Villiers and de Villiers (1978) suggest, this process is still not fully understood. It is clear, however, that the development of the meaning system of the language involves an interaction of the child's linguistic knowledge, knowledge about the non-linguistic context, and strategies used by the child in understanding or using a word.

Learning to communicate

Learning a language involves much more than learning the sound patterns, grammatical rules, and meaning of one's language; it also involves learning the rules of language use needed for communicating with others. The child must learn, for example, that the phrase "Can you pass the salt?" is not usually answered by saying "Yes, I can".

Learning to communicate includes the following areas, among others. Firstly, the child must learn conversational rules such as turn-taking, forms of politeness, and not presenting information which the listener already knows. Different codes of the language such as formal and informal styles and when these are to be used must also be learned. The child must also learn how to use language in a wide range of social acts such as the following:

- asking questions;
- making requests;
- giving orders;
- expressing agreement/disagreement;
- apologizing.

As was mentioned earlier, the process of learning conversational rules begins at an early age. The child's crying and the reaction of adults to this as well as the child's smiling and cooing to show contentment are forms of communication. Parents treat young infants as if they were *trying* to communicate, and through this the child learns conversational skills. As linguistic abilities develop, the child learns to use language in an increasing variety of social functions. Children also learn to vary their form of speech according to whom they are speaking with. For example, even four-year-olds have been found to adjust their speech when speaking to two-year-olds. The refinement of communicative skills continues throughout childhood.

Although it is clear that much of the social uses of language are learned through interacting with others, both adults and peers, it is not yet clear exactly how the child develops various communicative skills. Explanations of this process must take account of the development of a complex set of skills including the ability to analyse non-verbal aspects of the communication setting as well as the ability to use certain linguistic forms.

Conclusions

Although it is still not completely understood how children learn language, a large body of knowledge has accumulated in the area. What is the relevance of this knowledge for parents raising their children bilingually?

Among many parents, pre-school teachers and health-care personnel, one often hears the view that immigrant and minority group children will learn the minority language (as well as the majority language) simply by hearing it spoken around them. Such a view seems to reflect a theory of language development which sees the child as having an inborn ability to learn language and the role of adults as simply providing the input which activates this ability. Further research developments presented in this chapter, however, have indicated that adults play a much more active role than this in the child's language development.

Engaging the child in conversations in which input is provided about topics which interest the child, and where the parent is an active listener so that the child is motivated to talk, have been found to be highly important in the child's language development. This provides the foundation for "the negotiation of meaning", a process felt to promote language development, in which parent and child collaborate in the conversation, each expressing their ideas, needs, etc. Another "adult-related" process felt to be important for the child's progress in language development is "recasting" or expanding the child's utterances in a changed form which, nevertheless, reflects the central meaning of the child's utterance (Baker & Nelson, 1984). This process will be described further in Chapter 9.

Parents are also important in another way. We have earlier described the active role which the child plays in learning to structure and understand its environment, including language. Parents can greatly enchance this structuring process by exposing the child to a rich variety of experiences from which concepts can be developed and a picture of the world built up. It is not only the variety of experiences which is important but the way in which these match the child's level of development. Children learn mainly what they are ready to learn in their work of structuring the world. For example, with regard to language development, it has been suggested that the child progresses by understanding language which is just a little beyond its current stage of development, this occurring with the help of context (Krashen, 1981). This type of input is provided naturally when parents attempt to speak to their children as much as possible as well as aim towards communicating with their children.

Children also learn by modelling the behaviour of others. Here, not only adults are important, but also children speaking both the minority and majority languages.

Finally, language development, as an active and creative process on the part of the child, requires not only that the child receives stimulation, but also that it has time on its own. This is necessary in order for the child to be able to analyse its experiences, test out new ideas about how language functions, and practise newly acquired skills.

6 Learning two languages: simultaneous and successive bilingualism

In the previous chapter the language learning process in general was described. The present chapter focuses specifically on language learning in the bilingual child.

In general, bilingual children learn their two languages in one of two ways: either the languages are learned at the same time, usually from birth (i.e. *simultaneous* bilingualism) or one language is learned after the other (i.e. *successive* bilingualism). A common practice is to use the age of three as a cut-off point for distinguishing simultaneous and successive bilingualism. It should be pointed out at once that both simultaneous and successive bilingualism acquired during early childhood can lead to a high degree of bilingualism. There is no rule stating that one must learn two languages from birth in order to become bilingual. How well the child learns the two languages is probably more related to outside factors such as how favourable the environment is for learning and maintaining two languages than when a second language is introduced. Nevertheless, there is, of course, a big difference between introducing a second language at, say, the age of four and the age of ten.

The issue of successive bilingualism is thus also related to the question of *when* the majority language should be introduced. Research findings shedding light on this issue will be discussed later in the chapter. We will begin, however, by briefly describing the language learning process for the bilingual child who learns his two languages at the same time, and the child who learns them successively.

Simultaneous bilingualism

A number of studies have been carried out of children learning two languages from birth, in which different language combinations have been studied. To illustrate some general trends in these studies we will concentrate on one which gives a picture of bilingual development typical of that found in a number of other studies. In this particular study, which has become a classic in the field of early childhood bilingualism, Werner Leopold, a professor of German at an American university, described the language development of his German-English-speaking daughter, Hildegard, during the early years. Hildegard was exposed to German from her father and English from her mother while growing up in the United States.

In the beginning, Hildegard seemed to combine the two languages into one system. For example, the speech sounds she produced belonged to a single system which was not differentiated by language. In her early sentences she mixed English and German words and did not differentiate between the languages when speaking to monolingual speakers of each language. At the end of her second year, however, she began showing signs of beginning to separate the languages.

From the ages of two to five Hildegard's dominant language was English. She had difficulty in pronouncing certain German sounds and used very simple grammatical forms in that language, often with an English word order. When she was five, however, she spent half a year in Germany, and this visit had an enormous influence on her German. After a month in the German environment she had difficulty speaking English. After the return to the United States the opposite occurred, however. She quickly regained her fluency in English and began to have difficulties with German. After about half a year, however, this reaction to German was overcome and she could then be considered to be really bilingual (although clearly dominant in English).

As Grosjean (1982) points out there are a number of aspects of Hildegard's bilingual development which are frequently reported in connection with studies of other bilingual children as well. These are:

- an initial stage in which the child mixes the languages;
- a slow separation of the two languages;
- the influence of one system on the other;
- one of the two languages usually being dominant;
- a rapid shift in balance when input in the environment changes.

Similar patterns of development in bilingual and monolingual children

Although Hildegard was learning two languages, in general, the pattern of her language development was similar to that of a monolingual child. In other words, researchers suggest that the development of each of the bilingual child's languages follows the pattern of monolingual children's development who have this language as their only language. Thus, if certain forms are equally difficult in the two languages, they will appear at approximately the same time in the two languages; if a form is easier or more difficult in one of the languages, it will appear early or late, just as it does for the monolingual child.

In the last chapter, the tasks faced by the child in learning language were described. These tasks are, of course, no different for the bilingual child except for the fact that they need to be carried out in two languages instead of one. Thus, one often hears the view that the bilingual child has twice the work of the monolingual child. Although it is undoubtedly true that the bilingual child has more to learn about language than the monolingual child, it is questionable whether the child actually has twice the amount to learn. For one thing, most bilinguals are not equally fluent in two languages in all areas; instead, for most, there is a functional distribution between the languages so that, in some areas of the person's life, one language dominates, while in other areas the other language does. Another argument against the idea that the bilingual child has twice as much work as the monolingual child is the fact that although languages are different in many ways, they still have certain elements in common, e.g. in terms of meaning. Some researchers thus suggest that the "parts" of the two languages which are common to both are stored together in the brain.

Nevertheless, one must keep in mind that although the *pattern* of development in the bilingual's two languages is similar to that of the monolingual child, the *rate* of development may clearly not be. This is because the environment of the bilingual usually favours one language over the other. As was mentioned earlier, this situation is likely to have two effects: 1) development in one of the languages will be slower than that occurring in monolingual children learning this language as their first language; 2) the stronger language will influence the weaker one (i.e. interference will occur). If the environment provides equal exposure to the two languages (e.g. as may be the case in certain stable bilingual communities) these problems may not occur.

However, in one important way, the simultaneous bilingual child does differ from the monolingual child and this is that he/she has the task of learning to separate the two languages and to assign various words to each of the two language systems. Thus, rather than at the level of basic developmental processes involved in language acquisition, it is at this level that bilingualism can be stated to be more "difficult" than monolingualism. The "separation" process will be described in some detail so that parents will better understand the developmental stages which their children go through.

Learning to separate the languages

Many research findings suggest that the bilingual child's separation of the languages is a gradual process. As the child becomes more and more aware of the presence of two languages in its environment, the languages become more and more separated. In the following description of this process, examples from English-Swedish-speaking children (Arnberg, 1981) are used to illustrate several of the stages which the child goes through. Similarities have also been found with children learning other languages, however. Nevertheless, it is important to point out that the language combinations which have been studied so far are still limited so that the way in which specific languages may interact with one another is not completely clear at the present time.

Initially, the bilingual child does not appear to differentiate between the vocabularies of the two languages but has one system composed of words from each language. Some researchers suggest that there is little overlap in the words from each language; i.e. activities, objects, etc. are either named in one language or the other, but rarely in both. Other researchers, however, suggest that there is some degree of overlap in the two vocabularies during this stage. The speech material from a little boy named Danny can be used to illustrate this mixed vocabulary stage. At the time he was observed, Danny's language production consisted mainly of one-word utterances taken from either language. For example, he used the words "flygplan" ('aeroplane'), "doggie", "bye", and "bil" ('car') to both Swedish- and English-speaking people.

The child's early multi-word utterances also show a combination of words from both languages. Here are some examples from another Swedish-English-speaking child at 2½ years old, which illustrate typical utterances during this period:

Titta, bunny (*'Look, bunnie'*);
En block (*'A block'*);
En piggies till (*'A piggies more'*);
Här är budda (= butter) (*'Here is budda'*);
Horsie sova (*'Horsie sleep'*);
Är det ducks? (*'Is it ducks?'*).

Other ways in which the child uses the two languages during this period also seem to indicate that he is trying to combine them into a single system. For example, Grosjean (1982) points out the use of compounds and blends. In compounds the bilingual child uses the corresponding words in the two languages side by side, as if they were one word, e.g. "bitte-please" produced by a German-English-speaking child. In blends the child combines the two words into one, e.g. a French-English-speaking child's use of the word "pinichon", combining the English word "pickle" with the French word "cornichon".

As the child grows older, the two vocabulary and grammatical systems become increasingly differentiated. Researchers such as Volterra and Taeschner (1978), however, suggest that in order to help him separate the two languages, the child at first rigidly associates the languages with different speakers. There may be other reasons, however, why young children may insist on a strict classification of speakers according to what language they speak. Young children may have trouble understanding that a person can know more than one language or possess varying degrees of bilingualism, because the young child sees the world in more absolute terms. When the child's picture of the world is challenged, it, naturally, may become upset. Numerous examples from research studies do in fact show that, for whatever reason, young children often do become upset when addressed in the "wrong" language by a parent. This is illustrated in the following example from an English-Swedish-speaking child of two-and-a-half years old:

> **Child** (to English-speaking mother): Jag vill ha en SPOON. (*'I want a spoon'*).
> **Swedish-speaking father** (to child): Vill du ha en SPOON? (*'Do you want a spoon?'*).
> **Child** (upset): Nej, sked! (*'No, spoon'* (Swedish)).

Research findings from other studies also show the child's tendency to classify speakers according to language. For example, at the age of four Hildegard asked her mother, "Do all fathers speak German?" (Leopold, 1954). In a study of a Dutch-English-speaking child it was reported that the child, before the age of two-and-a-half, insisted that all women spoke English and all men Dutch, even when presented with contrasting examples (De Houwer, 1984). Many parents at this stage tell amusing stories about how they are only allowed to speak the "wrong" language if they pretend to be a person (or animal!) normally using that language, like a grandparent or dog from the minority language country. Volterra and Taeschner (1978) suggest that it is only when the child ceases to classify speakers in terms of their language that the child can be said to be truly bilingual.

Increased understanding of the use of the two languages with time

As time goes on children show increasing sophistication in their understanding of the difference between their languages and the situations in which each can be used. This is illustrated in the following delightful conversation with a five-year-old English-Swedish-speaking child:

English-speaking adult: "How do you know when to speak English and when to speak Swedish?"

Child: "*You* speak English. My daddy speaks Swedish and he also speaks a little English."

Adult: "Do you ever speak English at your day nursery?"

Child: "No."

Adult: "Why not?"

Child: " 'Cause that my Swedish talk. Then I speak Swedish. Then the others wouldn't know and the babies there wouldn't know so I will have to speak Swedish there."

Adult: "When you go to America – do you ever speak Swedish there?"

Child: "Yes, to mormor ('grandma') 'cause she's gonna come to us some day. When she says 'yes' and then it's 'ja' in Swedish."

Although this example shows that the five-year-old has quite a different understanding of his/her bilingualism than, say, the two-year-old, it should be recognized that even the older child has more to learn about using the two languages. For example, children at this age sometimes have trouble understanding that monolinguals cannot understand them when they speak one of their languages. In one case, a five-year-old was reported as only translating "difficult" sentences when reading a story to his monolingual cousin. Children at this age are also reported as having difficulty in carrying out tasks such as being told in one language to say something to someone in the other language.

How the child becomes aware of the two languages

It has earlier been suggested that the child mixes the languages because it is unaware of the presence of the two languages in its environment. As the child becomes more and more aware of its bilingualism, language mixing gradually disappears. How then does the child become aware of its bilingualism? Although researchers are not sure about exactly what factors are involved, several suggestions have been made:

- the child is helped by learning more and more about each language;
- the child uses clues about how words sound;
- the child uses information about the situation in which a word was first used;
- the child pays more and more attention to adult ways of using the languages as it gets older;
- social experiences in using the languages help the child to learn to separate them.

One important factor in explaining the separation process is undoubtedly the child's linguistic knowledge. As the child's knowledge of each language increases, it can be expected that this will help him in learning to differentiate between them. Phonological cues are also probably involved so that children classify words, as to which language they belong, according to how they sound. Children also use information about which language context the word was used in.

Another explanation is offered by the American researcher, Marilyn Vihman, who studied the bilingual development of her own English-Estonian-speaking children. This explanation is based on the research of the psychologist, Jerome Kagan, who has suggested that the young child becomes increasingly self-aware towards the end of the second year. As self-awareness increases the child becomes more and more sensitive to adult standards as well as more motivated to meet these standards. This increasing sensitivity to adult standards may be an important factor in the language differentiation process. Important here, however, would appear to be the language behaviour of the adult models. Do children whose "adult models" mix their languages show a delay in language differentiation when compared with children whose "adult models" are strict about separating the languages?

Another suggestion is related to the importance of the child's experiences in using the two languages. Seen in this way, learning that one is bilingual is similar to the learning of other concepts. In learning a new concept one needs both positive and negative feedback. Some research findings have shown how negative feedback, such as failing to communicate in a certain situation, may help the child in language separation. For example, in a study by Alvino Fantini of two children acquiring Spanish in the home and English in the outside environment, Fantini described how if the children made "a wrong language choice" to speakers, they were met by either no response, confusion, laughter, or amusement. It was suggested that these reactions encouraged the children to sort out the lexical items in relation to the persons addressed. Although this was first done on a trial and error basis, at a later stage the child paid more attention to the language which was heard from a particular source.

Some data from a study of English-Swedish-speaking children (Arnberg & Arnberg, in press) also give support to the suggestion that a failure to communicate may help the child to focus on its bilingualism. Parents of two of the children studied, who were found to have differentiated between the two languages at an extremely early age, both described their children as having experienced a "language shock". This had consisted of the children having attempted to communicate with their grandparents in the "wrong" language, this having led to an experience of extreme frustration. Following this experience, the children's awareness of the difference between the languages appeared to increase dramatically, and they subsequently spoke each language correctly to speakers of each language. This example illustrates the importance of exposing the bilingual child to a wide variety of language experiences and contacts with native speakers from both language groups in order to help the child become more aware of the presence of the two languages in its environment.

Why is bilingual awareness important?

Many parents may naturally wonder why it is important that the child be made aware of its bilingualism at an early age. Can one not just let this developmental process unfold on its own, so to speak? Although researchers do not fully understand the role bilingual awareness plays in the child's development of the two languages, one suggestion of practical concern is that progress in each language may be slowed down if the child has not learned to separate the languages. A so-far unexplored question concerns the following issue as well. As researchers such as Vygotsky (1974) have suggested, the pre-school years are critical with regard to the development of inner language and thinking processes. It is possible that the failure to separate the two languages may negatively influence development in this area.

The implications of this discussion are, naturally, that if bilingual awareness is shown to be important for the bilingual child's language and cognitive development, ways of helping the child to become aware of its bilingual situation need to be developed. That such training is possible is indicated by the fact that children who show an early awareness of their bilingualism often have parents who frequently talk about the difference between the languages with them or have had certain social experiences in connection with using their two languages. Such types of learning experiences could then be provided for all children.

Successive bilingualism

Up to this point the focus of the chapter has been on simultaneous bilingualism. Many children, however, especially in homes where both parents speak the minority language, may learn the languages successively, i.e. they are exposed to the minority language in the home and learn the second language (or the majority language) at a later stage, e.g. when placed in a day-care centre or when old enough to begin playing with other children outside the home. Another example of successive bilingual acquisition is the case of an immigrant family moving to a new country at the time when their children have already made some progress in learning their first language.

In contrast to simultaneous acquisition, the research questions connected with successive acquisition are different. Here, the child does not need to separate the languages or become aware of its bilingualism because he/she already knows one language. Thus, researchers have been interested in studying other issues such as how the knowledge of one's first language influences the learning of a second language, the developmental stages the child goes through on its way to mastering the second language, differences between individual children in their approaches to learning a second language, etc.

Explaining the child's errors

Although it was earlier believed that many of the errors which children made when learning a second language were caused by interference from their first language, more recent studies have focused on the similarities in error patterns between the second language learner and monolingual children learning the language as their first language. Thus, the errors that the child makes may not always be due to an influence from the first language but, instead, may reflect general developmental patterns in learning the language which are experienced by all learners. A third type of error may reflect neither the influence from the first language or general developmental patterns, but, instead, the specific situation of the second language learner, i.e. being forced to communicate in a language over which one does not yet have an adequate command. Such errors thus reflect the child's tendency to misapply the rules of the target language, e.g. through simplification or over-generalization of these rules, before they are mastered.

A number of studies have been carried out investigating second language learning in children, both more global studies looking at the language learning process in general, and studies looking specifically at the development of particular grammatical forms such as questions, negative forms, etc. A review of these studies would require a book on its own, and the interested parent is referred to the reading list at the end of the book. However, in general, it can be stated that a great deal of similarity has been found in the pattern of development between the second language learner and monolingual children acquiring the language as their first language, thus supporting the role of developmental errors in the child's second language learning. On the other hand, evidence of interference from the child's first language has also been found. Interference may occur especially in connection with the beginning stages of the learning of the second language, in cases where structures in the two languages are very similar, or in situations where the child is forced to use the second language at an advanced level before it is ready, e.g. in a classroom situation. Thus, it has been found that the child's mother tongue does play an important role in the learning of the second language, but in a more complex way than that which was assumed earlier.

Strategies used by the child in learning a new language

The appearance of several different types of errors in the child's second language learning suggests that several processes are involved. Rather than arguing for one type of explanation or another, researchers have, instead, tended to focus on the types of strategies children use in learning a second language. Children may resort to many types of "aid" when they learn a new language, such as using their first language, over-generalizing or simplifying rules, etc. Certain structures in the target language may be unique to that language and cause similar learning problems for all learners, regardless of their first languages. The learning of such structures may also reflect patterns of development in the monolingual child. In other cases, however, the child's first language may interact with the learning of the second language in specific ways. A strategy unique to the second language learner, however, is the use of formulas in which the child acquires phrases such as "You know what", "I wanna do it", etc. through imitation as unanalysed wholes to which a global meaning is attached. (This topic was also mentioned in Chapter 5). This strategy enables the child to quickly begin to communicate with others. It is only at a later stage that the individual constituents in these phrases are analysed and combined with other words in order to form new utterances.

Thus, as in other areas of child bilingualism, the picture of successive bilingualism is more complex than was earlier assumed, and much more research is needed before the various strategies used by the child are fully understood. Finally, it has also become clear from various research studies that there are substantial differences in the way in which individual children go about learning a second language.

In contrast to adults, who often stop at some stage in their learning of a second language, children usually go on to achieve native-like proficiency levels in the language. Nevertheless, this still requires that the child has adequate input in the second language and is motivated to learn it. For some reason, many people feel that children will "pick up" a second language under any circumstances, e.g. even when they may attend a mother-tongue programme at school, or live in a residential area where they have little contact with majority language speakers, etc. But it is also important to realize, given adequate input and motivation, that even for a child, learning a second language is an arduous and time-consuming task.

The reasons why the immigrant child goes on to achieve a high degree of proficiency in the new language while his parents are often left behind, still struggling with the language even after many years, has been widely debated. Some researchers argue for the role of physiological changes in the brain which take place between childhood and adulthood, while others suggest that the difference is due to social and psychological factors.

Deciding what to do

Having now given a general description of the process of acquiring two languages at the same time or in succession, we turn to the difficult question of which method is to be recommended to parents. It is, of course, realized that not all parents have a choice in the way in which they raise their children bilingually. For example, parents in the mixed-language family may not be fluent enough in any language except their own to be able to speak it to their children. Thus, such parents do not have the choice of, for example, only using the minority language in the home and, consequently, raising their children as successive bilinguals. Immigrant families, where both parents have the same native language, may not have the opportunity to expose the child to the majority language until it is old enough to begin having playmates outside the home. Thus, such parents may not have the choice of raising their children as simultaneous bilinguals. Nevertheless, in many cases, parents in both family situations *do* have a choice, and the question of what advice is to be given then becomes relevant. We will first consider the question of simultaneous versus successive introduction of the languages, i.e. up to the age of three. This will be followed by a discussion of, in successive bilingualism, the issue of *when* and *how* the second language should be introduced.

Simultaneous or successive bilingualism?

Unfortunately, conclusive research findings are not available, at the present time, which would help parents to choose between simultaneous and successive introduction of the two languages. For example, if answers were available to questions concerning whether simultaneous or successive bilingualism was actually easier for the child, whether one method resulted in less interference than the other, or whether simultaneous bilingualism had a positive effect on the development of certain thinking and conceptual skills, as is sometimes claimed, it would be much easier to advise parents. At present, all that can really be said is that there appear to be advantages with both simultaneous and successive presentation of the two languages. (In the following discussion it should be assumed that by waiting with one language in *successive* bilingualism it is the majority language which is being referred to.)

One of the main advantages with *simultaneous* bilingualism is that, as has been pointed out earlier, the young child is not really aware of its exposure to two languages in the beginning. This avoids the problem of the child being resistant to learning a new language when it already possesses an adequate means of communication, a problem sometimes mentioned in connection with successive bilingualism. Another advantage with simultaneous bilingualism may be that one takes advantage of the infant's ability to produce a wide variety of speech sounds, rather than waiting until some of these sounds have disappeared from the baby's vocal repertoire and thus must be relearned. A disadvantage sometimes claimed with simultaneous bilingualism, however, is that simultaneous presentation of two languages may be confusing for the child. Nevertheless, such confusion, if it occurs at all, has usually been found to be of short duration.

A major advantage with *successive* bilingualism is that the older child's greater knowledge about the world and about language in general, longer memory span, and more efficient ways of handling information, can be expected to be an advantage in learning a second language. On the other hand, the child may be resistant to having to do the work of learning a new language when it already possesses an adequate means of communication in the first language. Not only must new labels be attached to concepts which already have labels, but new grammatical forms must also be learned where a perfectly satisfactory means of expression already exists. Some researchers also suggest that, in successive bilingualism, the child must overcome the force of previously established habits, this problem being avoided in simultaneous bilingualism.

In the absence of clear-cut research findings, it is suggested that parents consider factors other than the advantages and disadvantages of simultaneous and successive bilingualism in their decision concerning how to expose the child to the two languages. These include the parents' fluency in each language, and the opportunities for exposure to the two languages outside the home, etc. These issues will also be considered again in the following chapters, where language strategies in the bilingual family, and general goals for the child's degree of bilingualism, are discussed.

Successive bilingualism: the introduction of the majority language

In successive bilingualism, the child is thus in a bilingual situation in which it has been exposed to only one of the languages, at least up to the age of three. The typical case which comes to mind is that of a young child in an immigrant or minority group family, in which the minority language is spoken exclusively in the home, and in which the majority of the family's social contacts are with relatives or other immigrants sharing a similar background. At what age, then, should the child in this situation be exposed to the majority language? In other words, should the parents "wait until the first language is established," as is sometimes claimed, before introducing the second language. (This will perhaps necessitate placing the child in a pre-school programme in the minority language.) Or should parents, instead, opt for a bilingual model in which the majority language is introduced as soon as possible? What research findings are available which shed light on this issue?

Arguments against "one language first"

A serious weakness with the argument that one needs to "establish one language first" before introducing another is, of course, the fact that many children are raised with two languages in the home. Such children do not appear to suffer in their emotional, social, or intellectual development as a result of their early bilingual upbringing. It should also be recognized that bilingualism is a much more common phenomenon than one realizes. Millions of children throughout the world are brought up bilingually, and research findings have shown that they are able to learn two languages at an early age, in situations where exposure to the two languages is available in the environment, and where attitudes are positive toward bilingualism, etc. Another argument against a strong "mother tongue approach" is the fact that children, especially at an early age, seem to be able to switch mother tongues rather easily as a result of, for example, moving to a new country. One would not expect such a result if the mother tongue played such an important role as is sometimes claimed.

Arguments in favour of "one language first"

It is not clear, however, whether researchers advocating the importance of establishing one language before introducing another, are referring to naturalistic settings, such as the above, in which language is learned through play or in the family, or more formal learning situations, such as that of the classroom. If it is classroom situations which are being focused on, it is true that children face many difficulties when placed in a learning situation in which they have an inadequate command of the language of instruction. Being in such a situation is difficult enough for an adult, and for children it must be far worse as the child has no way of analysing its feelings or dealing with them in a rational way. Research findings throughout the world thus support the idea of mother tongue instruction for children who are unfamiliar with the language of the classroom in the pre-school and school. There are a number of reasons for this, including the following:

1. Learning is more difficult in an unfamiliar language than in a familiar one and, consequently, the child may fall further and further behind in school.
2. The child's self-concept suffers when its language is not represented in an important institution of society, i.e. the school. A positive self-concept is essential for learning.
3. Teachers are likely to have unfair expectations of immigrant and minority-language children if they are placed in regular classrooms, comparing them with children who have spoken the language of instruction all their lives. (It is a well-known fact that teacher expectations are highly important for children's progress at school.)

Further support of the idea of "one language first" are recent research findings showing that, contrary to earlier assumptions, older children seem better at learning certain aspects of a second language than younger children, due to their superiority in memory functions, rule-learning and problem-solving ability, etc. Thus, it is not seen as a disadvantage to wait with the introduction of the second language.

Reasons for introducing the majority language as early as possible

It is thus firmly agreed that the child's mother tongue should be used as the medium of instruction in situations where the child has an inadequate command of the majority language, whenever this is possible. Nevertheless, this does not mean that the introduction of the second language (at least in a limited way) should be delayed. A serious problem with the idea that "older learners are better" is the fact that only a limited range of language skills has been examined. It is probably true that the older child, due to his/her superior cognitive skills and knowledge about the world, will out-perform the younger child in learning *some* aspects of a second language. Other aspects, however, may require many years of practice to master or may even be learned more easily by the younger child.

Components of second language learning

A useful way of explaining differences between older and younger learners is to try and separate language learning into a number of different skills, instead of looking at it as one single skill. If all these sub-skills are considered, it may turn out that the younger child is actually at an advantage in learning a second language in comparison with the older child. Unfortunately, research findings concerning how older and younger learners perform in a number of these areas is still limited, although a number of practical experiences and observations are available. Four general components are suggested:

1. *General cognitive component*

As was mentioned earlier, some aspects of language appear to be learned more easily by the older child. Because the older child has greater knowledge about the world and can handle information more efficiently than the younger child, it is expected that it will be superior in tasks where these skills are involved. For example, because the older child has a greater number of concepts than the younger child, it can be expected to be superior in vocabulary learning.

2. *Specific linguistic component*

Some aspects of language are not related to general cognitive skills but appear to be of a more specifically linguistic nature. One reason why young children may have an advantage in learning such skills is that they require time to learn and, thus, the earlier the start, the more time which is available for learning. For example, it was mentioned in Chapter 3 that in the acquisition of certain grammatical forms such as tense markers, negatives and prepositions, monolingual children performed better than bilinguals, indicating that bilinguals, because they had had less exposure to the second language, needed more time for learning. Thus, beginning at an early age allows the bilingual child greater exposure time.

It may also be the case that some language structures are actually easier for the young child to learn than the older learner. For example, Roger Brown (1973) suggested that structures such as articles are always learned by the child, while adult second language learners have great difficulty in using them correctly. One possible explanation for this may be the young child's greater use of imitation in language learning in which whole chunks (e.g. article plus noun) are processed in contrast to the adult's (or older child's) more analytical approach to learning.

3. *Emotional component*

Many adults learning a second language often state that they feel like actors and actresses when speaking the language, i.e. that the language somehow does not feel "a part of them". Such a feeling naturally influences a person's motivation to use and learn a second language because communication is not experienced as being as rewarding as when the mother tongue is used. Although little has been investigated concerning the role of emotional factors in learning a second language, one argument why young children may more easily be able to "develop a feeling" for the second language is because learning in young children occurs in a more "holistic" fashion than it does for the older learner, in which emotions are strongly integrated with the child's learning. In contrast, it is often claimed that older learners and adults learn a second language in a more analytic way.

4. *Pronunciation component*

Pronunciation is one area where research findings have shown an advantage for the younger child. For example, in a study of Spanish-speaking children from Cuba emigrating to the United States, it was found that the younger the child was when it entered the United States, the more native-like the child's pronunciation was judged to be.

5. *Other reasons*

A number of other reasons have also been suggested for introducing the second language as early as possible, including the following:

– the young child has less to learn in the second language than the older child in order to reach age norms (and, thus, be accepted by peers);
– learning in young children occurs in highly concrete situations, which has been found to be an advantage for second language learning;
– young children are often uninhibited and do not seem to become upset by making mistakes, not being able to express themselves adequately, etc.;
– the young child has more time than the older child for language learning because acquiring language and gaining knowledge about the world are the main activities of young children.

Finally, there is the fact that at least for the majority of immigrant and minority language children their world is a bilingual one. Although parents play the single most important role in young children's development, other factors are also important, such as the pre-school, school, community, peer group, etc. For the majority of immigrant and minority group parents, unless the group is extremely large, it will be impossible to meet all of the needs of the developing child entirely through the institutions which the minority language and culture represent. Thus, in order for the child's identity formation and other areas of development to progress normally, it is important that the child be able to communicate in the majority language from an early age.

Conclusions

On the basis of the information presented above, the following guidelines are suggested to parents:

1. *Begin with both lanugages as early as possible*

Children throughout the world grow up bilingually, and early bilingualism is not dangerous. Nevertheless, it requires that a few general rules be followed.

Naturalistic settings, such as those of the family and playground, seem to be positive ones for learning a second language. Parents need to realize, nevertheless, the importance of providing good language models for their children. It should also be recognized that learning a second language is never an easy task, even for a child.

The way in which the majority language should be introduced in the pre-school and school depends on the child's knowledge of this language when starting the programme and is related to the second rule, i.e.:

2. *Introduce language shifts gradually*

It takes time and effort to learn a new language, even if one is a child. Because language is a highly important tool for learning, this means that the child's learning will be handicapped if the language used at pre-school or school is not adequately understood. If the child is to be placed in a pre-school programme and does not understand the majority language well, a programme should be chosen in which the minority language is used, and where the second language is introduced gradually, whenever such a programme is available. If the situation cannot be avoided in which the child must be placed in a majority language programme, parents should at least try to ensure that there are other children in the same group who share the child's language or that the child has access to personnel who speak the minority language. If this is not possible (and in many cases it, unfortunately, is not), parents should be comforted by the fact that, although this is probably a difficult situation for all children, many seem to manage it well.

With regard to placement in majority language programmes for children unfamiliar with this language, it may also be the case that a language shift at certain ages may be particularly difficult for the child. For example, in a study by Ingegärd Gardell (1978) of children from abroad, adopted into Swedish families, it was found that the children's language development (in Swedish) at a later age was related to the age at which the child had moved to Sweden. Children who had moved before 18 months of age were less likely to show language difficulties than those who had moved when they were between the ages of 18 to 24 months. Similar results were also found in a study by Gunilla Svensson (1979), looking at the adjustment of young immigrant children when placed in a day-care setting where they did not have access to adults who understood their language. The results showed, again, that the age period of one to two years was especially critical.

Why is it that a language switch at this age is particularly difficult for the child? One explanation is offered by Gardell in the above study of adopted children. During the first years the child builds up a picture of the world through using its sensori-motor skills. When the child is between 18 to 24 months he has progressed so long in development that he is able to think in terms of inner concepts or symbols, based on passive vocabulary, which has been acquired through contact with the linguistic and cultural environment. The child, at this age, is just beginning to use words and to combine them into utterances, and requires a language environment in which there are adults present who are able to provide appropriate language stimulation. If this language stimulation is not available, for example, due to the fact that there are no adults present who understand the child's language, this may negatively influence the child's language development in a more long-lasting way than that occurring when the child has made lesser or greater progress in language development.

3. *Expose the child to both children and adults*
   who are native speakers of each language
   Children learn a great deal about language from playing with other children, but they also need to hear language from adults. One reason for this is because adults and children use language in different ways. For example, some researchers have described adults' speech to children as a series of "language lessons". In a study by an American researcher, Sabrina Peck, it was found that, from adults, children learn about the meaning of words and how to express their ideas. Adults also work harder than children do at trying to understand what the child is saying, posing many questions. Other children, however, seem better at engaging the child in language play in which the sounds and structures of the new language can be practised. Similar results were found by a Swedish researcher, Kerstin Nauclér (1985), who examined immigrant children's language use when interacting with other children and adults in a day-care setting. She concluded that *both* adults and other children were highly important in children's learning of a second language.

Thus, try and expose the child to other children *and* adults speaking the majority language beforehand, if it is to attend a pre-school in which this language will be used. Also, in the minority language, try to expose the child to both adults and other children who speak this language, especially those who are slightly older, whom the child can model.

7 Language strategies in the family

This chapter focuses mainly on the mixed-language family. In most cases, such families consist of one parent who is a native speaker of the majority language, while the other parent is a native speaker of the minority language. In some mixed-language families, however, each parent may speak a different minority language. In contrast to families where both parents speak the same minority language, the mixed-language family's language situation is more complex, this motivating the focus on this situation in the present chapter. Nevertheless, some of the information provided, such as ways of coping with the difficulty of maintaining a weaker language in the home, will be of interest to most bilingual families.

In this chapter I will first discuss what strategies are available to the bilingual family and describe research findings concerning what is known about the results of these strategies. The chapter will conclude with some advice concerning strategy choice.

Examples of different strategies

Table 3 shows the four strategies most commonly used by bilingual families. Note the relationship between these strategies and the discussion of simultaneous and successive bilingualism in the previous chapter. Thus, the one person/one language strategy and the mixed strategy are both examples of simultaneous presentation of the two languages. The home/outside language switch and the initial one-language strategies, on the other hand, are examples of successive presentation of the two languages. In addition, simultaneous and successive bilingualism may vary along another dimension, that is whether each language is consistently associated with one source or not. The reason for dividing up the strategies in this way is that it has often been claimed that it is important, when raising a child bilingually, that the child associates each language with a specific person, activity, etc. We will now look more closely at these strategies, as well as several others.

TABLE 3 *Strategy in relation to two variables: distinct vs. interchangeable sources of languages, and simultaneous vs. consecutive introduction of languages.*

Sources of languages	Introduction of languages	
	Simultaneous	*Consecutive*
Distinct	One person – one language	Home language different from majority language
Inter- changeable	Mixed	Initial one- language

Mixed strategy

In a mixed strategy the languages are used interchangeably by the parents although, in most cases, it is mainly the parent speaking the minority language who switches between the languages. When the two languages are used may depend on a number of factors, such as the topic of conversation, the situation, the speakers present, the location of the conversation, etc. The pattern of use of the two languages in the family may also vary at different points in time. For example, following a visit to the minority language country, some families may find that the use of the minority language by all family members increases. A mixed strategy is a common one in bilingual families and often results because the family wishes to be "natural" or because no specific decision has been made concerning how to use the two languages in the home.

Although the mixed method *is* probably the most natural method, its weakness is that when no provision for speaking the minority language is made, the majority language often dominates. Ramjoue (1980) suggests that if at least one of the parents does not speak the minority language consistently in the home, the child's bilingualism will be enhanced if this language can be used between the parents, or if the parent speaking the majority language speaks this language to the child at least part of the time.

One person/one language strategy

The one person/one language strategy was mentioned in research studies of child bilingualism as early as 1913 in a study by a French linguist, Jules Ronjat. Ronjat and his German-speaking wife, wishing to raise their son, Louis, bilingually, were advised by Ronjat's colleague, Grammont, to strictly follow a strategy in which each parent spoke their native language to the child. In this way, it was suggested that the child would learn to speak the two languages without "noticing it" and without exerting any special effort. Another reason often given for the method is that, by associating each language with a specific person, it is believed that the child is assisted in learning to keep the languages separated and to avoid mixing them. Other advantages are that the child receives adult input in each language and that each parent can use their own language in communicating with the child, in this way establishing a natural emotional relationship with the child.

A one person/one language strategy raises the question of which language should be used between the parents. Several variations can be observed in bilingual families (i.e. in situations where both parents know both of the languages). The parents may mix the languages when addressing one another, use only the majority language, use only the minority language, or each parent may even use their own language when addressing the other parent. Although I am unaware of any research findings supporting this, it is my opinion that the best results will be achieved if both parents use the minority language when addressing one another. In this way the child's exposure to the minority language is increased by hearing it spoken by both of the parents. In addition, the status of the language is raised to that of "family language" and this may increase the child's motivation to use it. Nevertheless, it is realized that, in many situations, this will not be possible, especially in the case when the minority language is not an international language such as English, French, German, Spanish, etc. Thus, it is also important to point out that the method will also work even if the majority language is spoken between the parents. If this is done, however, it is extremely important that the parent speaking the minority language be absolutely consistent in the use of this language to the child. If this is not done, the child will become unmotivated to use the minority language, and begin answering the parent in the majority language.

There are several problems which are often reported in connection with the method. Firstly, many parents suggest that it is difficult to carry out the strategy if both parents are not bilingual because it results in one of the parents being excluded from the conversation at times. Most often this involves the majority language parent who does not understand or speak the minority language. This is, of course, an issue which must be considered by each individual family. In some cases, the majority language parent may choose to learn the other parent's language, at least to the extent that he/she is able to understand this language. This will also greatly enhance trips, which the family may make to the minority language country, for the entire family.

I have seen very different attitudes among parents with regard to their interest in learning their partner's language, even when this language is not an international language. Some parents state that they find it natural to learn the language of their partners while others feel that, unless the language is an international one, the pay-off for the time and energy required to learn a second language is simply too limited. On the other hand, some research findings from Wales have suggested that it is not so much the non-bilingual parent's knowledge of the other language but, rather, his/her attitude toward the other parent speaking it which is important. Thus, if the majority parent maintains an interested and supportive attitude toward his/her partner speaking the minority language to the child, this may be a highly important factor in raising the child bilingually. If, however, it is the case that a parent feels extremely uncomfortable in the situation of having a language used in the home which is not understood, the minority-language-speaking parent may prefer to use this language only when alone with the child.

A second problem concerns the difficulty of maintaining consistency at all times. There are many situations in which it is difficult to avoid using the majority language in front of the child, e.g. when talking on the telephone, at the child's day nursery, when friends or relatives are present who do not understand the minority language, or when the child has playmates over who only speak the majority language. In this latter situation, many parents state that they do not wish to give two sets of instruction or to embarrass their child by "singling him out". (Many parents state that they become used to speaking the minority language to the child even in the presence of others, however.)

Many parents also question whether it is absolutely necessary to be consistent at all times. Ramjoue (1980) suggests that the answer to this question is No, provided that the child can identify the reason for the parent having switched to the other language. For example, many children will accept the explanation that "mummy must speak 'language X' now because Grandma doesn't understand 'language Y'" and then be able to accept the parent switching back to "language Y" when alone with him/her again. Furthermore, the importance of absolute consistency has often been suggested in connection with the beginning stages of bilingual development because it helps the child to learn to separate the languages. Although it is also important in helping to maintain the two languages, a more important factor in bilingual maintenance is probably the child's total exposure to each language. Thus, after the language separation process is completed, families may wish (when necessary) to exercise greater flexibility in the use of the languages, while at the same time trying to provide as much total exposure to each language as possible.

A third commonly-occurring problem is the child's refusal to answer the parent in the minority language, this often occurring when a parent has not been absolutely consistent in using this language to the child. When the parent is inconsistent the child learns that the parent knows the majority language and, therefore, may become unmotivated to speak the minority language to him/her. This interaction pattern, i.e. of the child responding to the parent in the majority language, may even develop on a more unconscious level and is really difficult to avoid. For example, a young child may say something like "thirsty" in the majority language, to which the parent naturally responds by getting the child something to drink. This may, however, have the same effect, in the child's eyes, as if the parent had actually used the majority language. Thus, from an early age the child may develop a habit of responding to the parent in the majority language.

Some parents state that they deal with the above problem by pretending not to understand the child or not responding unless the "right" language is used. On the other hand, other parents react very strongly against such methods, as they feel this may irritate the child or cause the child to distrust the parent. Although such actions may seem unnatural, it should be recognized that a firm attitude on the part of the parents will probably have a positive effect on the child's use of the minority language. At any rate it should be realized that simply reminding the child to use the minority language is often effective.

The key issue here, regardless of which approach is taken, is to, in any way that the parent can, give the child an incentive for speaking the minority language. This can be done in a number of ways, such as making it a necessary condition in order to converse with the parent as above, or by making it fun or "special" to speak the minority language with the parent and others through the use of, for example, games, special activities, books, and records in the minority language, etc. Without such an incentive, children often seem to lack motivation to use the minority language, although motivation may increase at times, e.g. in connection with trips to the minority language country.

The problem of the child responding to the minority-language-speaking parent in the majority language is likely to be greater if the child attends a majority language pre-school programme than if the child is cared for at home by the minority-language-speaking parent, or attends a day-care programme in which the minority language is used, etc. There are several reasons for this. Firstly, if the child speaks the majority language all day long, it is likely that this language will become dominant and actually be easier for the child to speak. Research findings, such as those of Stanislav Dorniç at Stockholm

University, have shown that many adult immigrants find it more tiring, and to be a greater strain, to speak a second language than their mother tongue. It is likely that the situation is similar for the child, especially after a long day. Furthermore, all of the child's activities during the day have been carried out in the majority language, resulting in the lack of vocabulary in the minority language for concepts related to the activities experienced. It may also be difficult for young children to switch back and forth between languages because they do not have the same degree of consciousness about their two languages as older children and adults have. Difficulty in switching between the languages can even occur among adults, however; this is often related to situations involving "mental overload" such as stress or fatigue.

If all attempts to get the child to speak the minority language fail, the parents should never give up the attempt to raise the child bilingually. They should, instead, continue to consistently speak the minority language to the child, in this way helping the child to continue to learn to understand the language and to receive valuable ear training in connection with it. Most children do not seem to be bothered by the typical dual language conversations which result from this strategy. Parents often find that, given this background, many children adjust quickly during visits to the minority language country and make rapid progress during these visits. It is not advisable, however, to force the child to use the minority language, but rather, the parent should try to increase the child's own motivation for speaking the language. Forcing the child may cause the child to form negative attitudes towards the language, which may even decrease motivation to use it at a later stage.

Both parents speaking the minority language

In some homes where both parents are highly fluent in the minority language, both may decide to speak this language to the child in order to balance the dominating influence of the majority language from the outside environment. This is, of course, a highly positive situation for fostering bilingualism in the home (similar to the situation in which both parents share the same minority language) due to the high degree of exposure the child receives in the minority language. It is also less likely in such families than in those where the parents choose a one person/one language strategy, that the child will respond to the minority-language-speaking parent in the majority language, due to the use of the minority language as the only family language. Nevertheless, when this strategy is adopted by the *mixed-language* family, researchers have suggested that there may be several long-range difficulties which parents should consider.

One difficulty concerns how the majority language parent will feel about speaking the minority language to the child as the child grows older and becomes increasingly influenced by the majority society. Another problem is that if the family decides to leave the majority language country, no provision will have been made for maintaining the majority language in the home and, thus, this language may be lost in the new country (Ramjoue, 1980).

Another factor to consider, which was mentioned in Chapter 6, concerns the child's need of contact with both children and adults in learning the majority language. If the child has the opportunity for frequent contact with majority-language-speaking relatives or other adults, the choice of this strategy may not pose a problem; if this is not the case, however, and the child is to attend a majority language pre-school or school, parents may wish to consider this factor.

Also when using this strategy, as with the one person/one language strategy, parents sometimes question how important it is to be absolutely consistent. For example, in one family I interviewed, the majority-language-speaking father (who had chosen to speak the minority language to his child and felt highly comfortable in doing so) stated that he regretted not being able to sing to the child in his own language. (The father was a musician and music was an important part of his life.) Rather than depriving the child of such an emotionally and intellectually rewarding experience, it is felt that in such cases an exception should be made, explaining to the child what the reasons for this are.

Initial one-language strategy

As was mentioned earlier, some parents feel that it is confusing for a young child to learn two languages at the same time. The approach is usually for both parents to speak the majority language to the child and introduce the minority language after the child has "learned" the majority language. In most cases, parents usually try to introduce the minority language between the ages of three and five. This, however, introduces the problem of one of the parents having to use a new language in addressing the child than that which was used earlier. Since emotional bonds between parent and child are built up via language, children are highly resistant to a parent speaking a new language to them in this way, although young children may be more sensitive to this than older children. Thus, it is difficult to recommend this method on these grounds. Furthermore, as has been mentioned in early chapters, there is little support for the idea that learning two languages simultaneously is, in fact, confusing for the child.

Parents who choose to postpone the introduction of the minority language because they feel that it will be easier to introduce it at a later age, should stop and think a moment. From a motivational point of view, unless there is a great deal of support for the minority language in the outer environment, children are probably less likely to be motivated to use it, after they have already learned to communicate in the majority language, than they would have been at an earlier stage when they were not really aware of the presence of the two languages in their environment. Also, older children are more influenced by the language of the peer group than younger children.

Both parents speaking the majority language

In some cases both parents may decide to speak the majority language to the child, although, even in this situation, the parents wish the child to become bilingual. There may be several reasons for this. The minority language parent may have lived in the majority language country for many years and feel very comfortable speaking the majority language. Parents may also feel that it will be confusing speaking two languages in the home, fear that the child's learning at school will suffer if the majority language is not spoken in the home, or not wish to exclude one of the parents from conversations. Some parents may even feel that their own adjustment to, and integration in, the majority language country is of greater importance than the child's bilingualism.

Although it is not the purpose of this book to discourage minority language parents from speaking the majority language to their children if they wish to do so, several points are important to consider. As is the case with the majority parent choosing to speak the minority language, it is highly important that the parent be highly fluent in his/her second language. Unless this is the case, it may be difficult to establish a natural emotional contact with the child. The Swedish child language researcher, Ranghild Söderbergh (1979), suggests that through language one expresses one's feelings and one's total self. It is felt that this is difficult to do in a language over which one does not have a good command. Another factor related to fluency is the fact that children may lose respect for a parent who speaks a language over which they do not have an adequate command. A second factor to consider is the fact that if the parents *do* wish the child to eventually become bilingual, this method has not been proven to be very effective, unless it is the case that there is a major source of input in the minority language outside the home.

Ramjoue (1980) suggests that since, from her experience, many parents may later regret their decision to speak the majority language to the child and wish to switch to the minority language, parents should ask themselves the following questions before deciding upon this strategy:

1. Will I always want to speak the majority language with my child or will I regret his missing out on books and songs in the minority language, and certain aspects of the minority language culture, etc.?
2. Will the child be placed in many situations, such as vacations in the minority language country or visits from grandparents, where being bilingual is important and not being so might make the child feel uncomfortable?
3. Will the child later resent the lost opportunity for becoming bilingual?

If the parents do wish to adopt the minority language at a later point in time, experience has shown that this is difficult once the emotional and language links have been established between parent and child. It may be somewhat easier to do this following an extended visit to the minority language country. The parent can also begin to introduce the minority language gradually through games and songs, setting aside a certain time of the day for reading stories or listening to records in the minority language, etc. But parents should, nevertheless, realize that these approaches, although they may be helpful, can never be equivalent to the active use of the minority language in the home from the beginning.

Strategies based on other factors

Other strategies have also been reported in the literature, based on factors such as time, location, activity, etc. For example, in some "time strategies" the minority language is spoken in the morning, the majority language in the afternoon, or a certain day of the week may be set aside for using the minority language, etc. Some families may adopt a "location strategy", e.g. an "upstairs/downstairs" strategy in which the minority language is spoken upstairs (or in certain rooms of the house), and the majority language spoken downstairs, etc. Finally, there may be the strategy of using the minority language during certain activities such as eating dinner. Experience has shown that strategies such as these often tend to break down because they are unnatural.

Research findings on the effects of strategies

Research findings concerning the effects of various strategies in raising the child bilingually have not been very conclusive. One reason for this is because it is difficult to ensure that families differ on strategy alone. For example, in some cases a family using a mixed strategy may achieve better results than one using a one person/one language strategy because, in the first case, the family has had the opportunity to travel frequently to the minority language country, receive extended visits from relatives, etc. while, in the second case, such trips or visits have been infrequent.

Nevertheless, observations from many bilingual families seem to suggest that it does "pay off" to consistently use the minority language in the home, either in the form of a one person/one language strategy or by only using the minority language in the family. All factors being equal, families who provide consistent input are more likely than those who do not to have children who actively use the minority language. Nevertheless, the problem remains of determining whether the successful results are due to the strategy or whether other characteristics of "consistent" parents have also played a part.

For example, a number of research findings have suggested that it is difficult to maintain a one person/one language strategy in the home. In one such study of English-Swedish-speaking families (Arnberg, 1981), many English-speaking mothers stated that they found it difficult to consistently use the minority language when addressing the child. The conclusion to be drawn here is that if a one person/one language strategy is difficult to carry out, it could be the case that those parents who manage to successfully use the strategy may be different from other parents in certain ways which have importance for the degree of bilingualism achieved. For example, such parents may be more highly motivated, more disciplined, etc. than other parents. Thus, it could be these outside factors which are contributing to the results as well as the strategy itself.

Some research findings support this idea. For example, in a Canadian study it was found that English-French-speaking mothers selecting a one person/one language strategy in raising their children bilingually had a higher degree of education than other mothers in the study. Also, in connection with some of the earlier studies of parents successfully using this method, it has been suggested that in several cases the parents had a highly authoritarian style in bringing up their children.

Conclusions

In this final section I will try to summarize what has been presented in the chapter by giving some advice concerning choice of strategy in the bilingual family.

In deciding what strategy to use in raising one's child bilingually, both practical issues such as the parents' fluency in each language as well as other issues such as the family's needs with regard to proficiency in the two languages need to be considered. Selection of strategy must also be seen in relation to the child's total exposure to each language, e.g. the opportunities to participate in minority language pre-school and school programmes, to visit the minority language country on a regular basis, to meet other children and adults who speak the minority language, etc.

Thus, although it is difficult to recommend one strategy for all families, due to the fact that each individual family situation is different, I would nevertheless like to attempt to make some recommendations concerning what I believe to be the ideal situation for many mixed-language families. These recommendations are based on research findings, observations in bilingual homes, conversations with parents, and my own personal views.

I believe that the ideal situation is one in which parents consistenly follow a one person/one language strategy and where the minority language is spoken between the parents and used as the family language, whenever possible. If this is not possible, it is highly advantageous if the non-bilingual parent can at least learn to understand his/her partner's language to some extent. This greatly increases flexibility in the family with regard to language use, makes visits to the minority language country an enjoyable experience for the entire family, and provides good bilingual models for the child (i.e. the child sees that both parents are positive toward bilingualism). The parents should try to be as consistent as possible in each speaking their own language to the child. However, it is important to remember that even an inconsistent approach is better than no approach at all!

Although I would not discourage parents who wish to adopt the minority language as the only family language from doing so, I feel that in many cases parents do not possess the degree of proficiency necessary to be able to be as natural and spontaneous in their communication with the child as they would have been had their native language been used. Furthermore, although I do believe that children learn much of the majority language from playmates and others in the surrounding environment, I feel that interaction with an adult who is highly familiar with the child and highly invested in the child's progress cannot be overestimated. In conclusion, it is felt that by using the above strategy parents will achieve the following benefits:

- take advantage of an early start in introducing both languages;
- communicate naturally with the child in their own language;
- provide the child with adult input in each language;
- provide correct pronunciation in each language;
- maintain respect from the child toward the parent by each parent producing accent-free and fluent speech;
- provide exposure to both languages.

8 Family goals with regard to degree of bilingualism

In the preceding chapters we have discussed issues such as when the majority language should be introduced and, in connection with the mixed-language family, different ways of using the two languages in the home. A final issue concerns goals with regard to the child's degree of bilingualism, i.e. how proficient the child should be in each of the languages.

To many parents this may seem like an odd way of putting things. Naturally, most parents would like their children to be as proficient as possible in both of their languages. Although most immigrant and minority group children develop native-like proficiency levels in the majority language, as has been mentioned frequently, attaining a high degree of proficiency in the minority language is more difficult. Raising children bilingually has been shown to require a great deal of effort from parents, and some parents, naturally, may place a higher priority on this area than others. At the same time, most parents do wish their children to become bilingual. Thus, it may be useful to regard bilingualism in terms of different levels which parents can aim toward. These levels will be discussed separately for the mixed-language and single-language immigrant and minority group family.

Goals in the mixed-language family

In many mixed-language families, a continual problem is getting the child to actively use the minority language. In many situations where the child continually responds to the parent in the majority language, parents, unless they are highly motivated to raise their children bilingually, feel that they are fighting a losing battle and begin speaking to the child more and more often in the majority language. As was mentioned earlier, it is important that parents

Start speaking, playing, and interacting with the baby in your own language from the very beginning

Interaction and communication with others meaningful to the child are highly important for language learning

Children learn a great deal through imitation

realize that this attitude is wrong. Children are not failing to learn the minority language just because they do not speak it. They are actively listening to the language and storing up information about it. When the child *does* become motivated to use the language (and most children do, e.g. in connection with learning to read in the minority language, visiting relatives in the minority language country, participating in summer camp programmes in the minority language, etc.), many parents are amazed at the rapid progress which is made. My own research findings have supported this as well as those of other researchers. For example, McLaughlin (1984) reports a case of a five-year-old child who had grown up in Germany but had been exposed to English by his American father. Although the child had never spoken English, upon entering a kindergarten programme in the United States, the child was immediately able to speak English although many errors were made.

Progress is likely to be far less rapid during visits to the minority language country, however, if parents stop speaking the minority language to the child altogether. One reason for this is because language learning is felt to have an "incubation period". Remember that in Chapter 5 it was mentioned that children do not begin producing language until they are about one year old. Researchers suggest that this is because there is a period of learning to comprehend the language before speech occurs. If the child needs to do all the "comprehension work" upon arrival in the minority language country, parents may find that the child does not actually begin speaking until it is time for the family to return home!

The point to be made here is that language learning (and bilingualism) are ongoing processes. In other words, parents need to develop a long-range perspective with regard to their children's bilingualism. Continued input in the minority language, accompanied by regular visits to the minority language country, may ultimately lead to a fairly high level of proficiency in this language, although this may not be immediately evident.

The parents continuing to speak the minority language to the child on a consistent basis (although the child may not respond in this language) will be referred to as *passive* bilingualism and this represents the first goal. The second goal is called *active* bilingualism because the child is expected to use the minority language on a more active basis. The third goal is called *absolute* bilingualism and aims toward an equal or near-equal proficiency in both languages. It is, of course, realized, in connection with absolute bilingualism, that it is difficult to achieve native-like proficiency levels in a minority language in a situation where this language is not used in the wider environment. Nevertheless, I have met individuals having grown up in a monolingual country who appear to be highly proficient in both of their languages.

The above goals should be understood in the following way. Parents should aim for as high a degree of biligualism as they wish to, realizing at the same time that absolute bilingualism will require a great amount of time and effort to achieve, especially if there is little opportunity to use the minority language outside the home, e.g. in connection with the child's schooling. No research findings have indicated that this level of bilingualism is in any way "dangerous" for children. However, if parents feel that they are unwilling to exert the time and energy necessary to aim toward absolute bilingualism, rather than giving up the attempt to raise their children bilingually altogether, it is suggested that they aim for a lower level. The three goals for bilingualism are described in greater detail below.

TABLE 4 *Hypothetical goals for the bilingual education of pre-school-age children in the home*

Goal	Description	Parental activity level
1. "Passive" bilingualism	The child comprehends the minority language although he/she may not speak it.	The parent continues to speak the minority language to the child and encourages it to at least hear this language as much as possible even if the child may not speak it. Through nursery rhymes, songs, or games the child may be given training in pronouncing difficult sounds.
2. "Active" bilingualism	The child, in addition to comprehending the minority language, is also expected to be somewhat proficient in its production.	In order to encourage minority language production, both parents may use this language in the home, or the parent natively speaking it may actively encourage the child to use this language at all times. An effort is made to increase the child's opportunity to speak the minority language with native speakers both in- and outside the home. The child is exposed to the minority language as much as possible through books, records, games, etc.
3. "Absolute" bilingualism	The child possesses native-like, or near native-like, proficiency in both languages.	The minority language will probably have to be the language used in the home, unless some type of bilingual school programme is available. The parents employ more direct educational methods such as teaching the child literacy skills in the minority language, setting aside certain times of the day for language training, etc. As much time as possible should be spent in countries where the minority language is spoken. The parents may also be able to borrow video cassettes of children's television programmes from relatives. Extra training in the majority language, however, may be necessary if the child is to attend a majority language school. It would be highly desirable, however, to place the child in some type of bilingual programme, if one exists.

Passive bilingualism

A passive bilingual approach suggests that an understanding of the minority language is good ground on which to build more active skills at a later stage when the child becomes more motivated on its own. Although the child's speaking of the minority language should, thus, never become a prerequisite for the parent/parents continuing to speak that language to the child, the child is, of course, encouraged to do so at all times. Difficult sounds in the minority language may be practised by using nursery rhymes and songs. Many children enjoy participating in such activities even when they do not use the language more actively during ordinary conversations.

Advantages of passive bilingualism

One of the main advantages with a passive approach is that it makes maximal use of the child's and parent's motivation. By waiting until the child is motivated on its own, the parent's motivation for stimulating the child in the use of the minority language can be more effectively used. Such an approach also most closely approximates "normal development", as it emphasizes the child's development in the language of the peer group and school. There is little risk that the child will not be proficient in the majority language if the parent speaking this language makes a special effort to converse with the child, explain things to the child, and read to the child as much as possible.

In a way, one might even suggest that a passive approach may be more "risk-free" than other methods, although no specific research findings are available on this point. Many researchers working in the area of early childhood development emphasize the importance of the first five years of life for subsequent learning and development. An argument against a highly active bilingual approach during this period is that, because the child has so much to learn, it may be unwise to add the extra burden of achieving a high level of proficiency in a second language at this time.

Disadvantages of passive bilingualism

The main disadvantage with a passive approach is summed up by Barry McLaughlin (1984) who suggests the possibility that children who are exposed to a language only passively may not have the same grasp of the language as children who use it more actively. In other words, the way in which passive skills transfer to active skills is still poorly understood. Follow-up studies of children learning their two languages actively and passively will be necessary in order to shed light on this issue.

Active bilingualism

An active bilingual approach during the early years assumes that some degree of use of the minority language during early childhood benefits later proficiency in this language. Some support of this idea was given in Chapter 6 in the discussion of the time factor in learning a second language. There it was mentioned that many aspects of learning a second language take time to master; thus, the earlier start the better. An active approach can, likewise, be seen in terms of allowing more time for the mastery of certain language skills.

Advantages of active bilingualism

The main advantage with an active approach is, thus, that it provides greater assurance than with a passive approach that the child will be proficient in the minority language. The child's active use of the minority language is also likely to have a stimulating effect on the parent using this language. Another advantage may be related to pronunciation; i.e. by actively using the minority language the child may more easily be able to offset the dominating influence of the majority language, thus avoiding "having an accent" when speaking the minority language.

Disadvantages of active bilingualism

One of the disadvantages with an active method is that the risk is greater than with a passive approach that language learning will take away time from learning other important skills. However, the risk for this is still less than with an absolute approach.

Absolute bilingualism

An absolute bilingual approach, of course, assures that the child will be bilingual at a later age. Aside from the many positive aspects of being bilingual, bilingualism may actually be a necessity for some families. This may be the case, for example, if the family is undecided with regard to which country they will be living in in the future, travels frequently to the minority language country, or has relatives living in the majority language country who do not speak the majority language fluently.

Advantages of absolute bilingualism

The main advantage with an absolute bilingual approach is that the many positive aspects of being bilingual are experienced at an early age. An indirect advantage with the method may be that achieving a high degree of bilingualism at an early age requires that the parents must spend a great deal of time with the child, this being a positive factor in itself.

Disadvantages of absolute bilingualism

The main disadvantage with an absolute bilingual approach is the possible risk that the energy required for learning two languages really well may take away time from learning in other areas important in the child's development. This possible risk may be minimized, however, if parents are aware of this problem, helping the child to structure its "non-language learning time" effectively. This can be accomplished, for example, by providing stimulating activities for the child to participate in while playing alone, etc.

Goals in the single-language family

In the single-language immigrant or minority group family, the situation is not unlike that in the mixed-language family in that, frequently, the majority language becomes the child's dominant language. In contrast to the situation in the mixed-language family, however, it is less likely that passive bilingualism will result; rather, it is expected that the child will become an active bilingual due to the fact that in most families, the minority language is used exclusively in the home.

Thus, in the single-language family, the choice is mainly between active and absolute bilingualism. Which of these goals the family chooses is a highly individual matter. In some immigrant families the child's learning of the majority language will be given the highest priority (i.e. active bilingualism will be the goal) while in others, the family may feel that it is important for the child to achieve as high a level of proficiency as possible in both languages (i.e. absolute bilingualism may be the goal).

In some situations in the single-language family, however, the opposite may occur, i.e. the minority language may become the child's dominant language. This situation may arise, for example, if the minority language is the only language used in the home, the child attends a pre-school programme where the minority language is the main language of instruction, and the family lives in a neighbourhood where there is little contact with majority language speakers. The danger with the situation, however, is that the child may not develop native-like proficiency in either language. This is due to the fact that it is highly difficult to achieve native levels of proficiency outside of the country where a language is normally used. (This may be less true, however, in situations in which the minority language group is extremely large or in stable bilingual settings where each of the languages is used in certain domains of life.) At the same time, however, the child's contact with the majority language is too limited for the child to develop a native-like proficiency level in this language. It is felt that this situation, i.e. in which the child is not really perfect in either language and does not feel that it is a fully-fledged member of either ethnic community, is a highly difficult one for the individual and should be avoided at all costs. In such situations it is felt that parents should encourage the use of the majority language as much as possible outside the home while, at the same time, encouraging the child to identify with the minority language and culture.

Deciding upon goals for raising the child bilingually

The choice of goals with regard to the child's degree of bilingualism is naturally up to each individual family. A brief questionnaire has been constructed in order to help families in their consideration of which goals they may wish to aim towards, in which the total input in each language available both in the home and in the outside environment is considered. The questionnaire appears in the Appendix.

Bilingual education

In many countries throughout the world it has become a more and more common phenomenon that both parents work outside the home, thus leaving the care of even young children to others. Immigrant and minority group children may participate in pre-school programmes in which the majority language, the minority language, or both languages are used. As pre-school programmes are an important complement to parents in raising children bilingually, they must also be considered in the discussion of overall family goals with regard to degree of bilingualism.

Although, in general, the language models available for pre-school education for immigrant and minority language children vary from country to country, the following models are frequently represented:

- regular majority language programmes with or without personnel who speak the minority language;
- programmes carried out in the majority language but which are especially designed to meet the needs of immigrant and minority group children (sometimes referred to as "immersion" programmes);
- bilingual programmes;
- programmes in which only the minority language is used;
- minority language play-groups.

Probably the most frequent type of pre-school programme for the immigrant and minority group child is one in which the child is placed in a regular majority language programme. In this situation the child may or may not have access to personnel who speak the minority language, the former being, of course, most desirable. A common problem in many countries is the large number of minority languages represented by immigrant and minority group children, making it virtually impossible to always have available to the child personnel who speak their language. I have seen several ways of handling this problem, including the use of parallel curriculum materials in various languages in the form of tape-recordings of children's songs, stories, etc. and the use of parent volunteers in the programme who represent various languages and cultures, etc.

A second model is one in which, although the majority language is used, the programme is specifically designed to meet the needs of the immigrant or minority language child. This includes having bilingual teachers who at least understand the child's language although they may not use it, allowing children to use the minority language until they are able to communicate in the majority language, and employing personnel who are sensitive to the child's cultural background, etc. A third model is bilingual models in which both the minority and majority languages are used. Such programmes may include majority language children (two-way bilingual programmes) or minority language children only (one-way programmes). Another type of model, especially common in Sweden, is mother tongue programmes in which only the minority language is used. Finally, mother tongue play-groups may be organized by immigrant organizations, parents, etc. In contrast to other types of programme, these often emphasize a high degree of parent involvement. The starting of mother tongue play-groups will be considered in greater detail in Chapter 10.

It should be recognized, however, that parents may not always have a choice among various models. In many communities, there may be too few children from one single language group to start a programme. But it is also important to emphasize that parents can themselves be active in influencing authorities to start the types of programme which they desire. They may even include other models than those mentioned above.

Research findings

Research findings have not given a very conclusive picture of the effects of various models. Such studies are difficult to carry out because even the same model type can vary from one community to another. Furthermore, children enter the programme with varying skills in each of their languages, teachers vary in the extent to which they are trained to meet the specific needs of the immigrant and minority group child, and some parents may have chosen the model while others have not, etc. Nevertheless, a general (and hardly surprising) trend seems to be that the more the minority language is used in the programme the better the child's proficiency in this language becomes. Bilingual programmes, in contrast to mother-tongue-only programmes, have the advantage that both languages are used in the programme. However, unless teachers are very aware of this problem, a common trend in such programmes is that the majority language dominates, especially if majority children are enrolled in the programme. (This problem is of course related to the underlying status of each of the languages in the surrounding community.)

Choosing a pre-school model

In the choice of pre-school model there are really two issues which parents need to consider:

1. the child's skill in each language when starting the programme;
2. the family's overall goals with regard to the child's degree of bilingualism.

With regard to the first issue, parents are referred to the discussion at the end of Chapter 6. With regard to the second issue, parents need to consider their goals for raising the child bilingually, especially in relation to how much input is available in each of the languages in the child's total environment. For example, if only the minority language is spoken in the home, parents may wish to choose a pre-school programme in which the majority language is spoken, at least for part of the time. On the other hand, if the majority language dominates in the home, parents may wish to support the minority language by placing the child in a minority language pre-school programme. At the same time, parents should recall the earlier discussion concerning the importance of introducing language shifts gradually, thus avoiding placing the child in a classroom situation in which the language of instruction is not understood. Thus, parents also need to plan ahead in terms of which models will be available when the child begins school. Thus, if the child will be placed in a majority language programme when it begins school, this is good reason to introduce this language as early as possible.

Conclusions

The present chapter has focused on various goals for families raising their children bilingually with regard to children's degrees of proficiency in the two languages. In addition, there are several other factors I would like to mention, regardless of which goal is chosen. These include the following:

1. *Make sure that the child is good
   in at least one of the languages*

   Bilingualism is a positive thing but it must not result in the child not knowing either of the languages really well, i.e. the child must have at least *one* good language. (This of course does not mean that the child cannot have two good languages.) This is because language is an extremely important tool for learning, thinking, identity development, etc.

   The child's dominant language should, in my opinion, be the language in which it will attend school. This is because research findings have shown a correlation between success at school and knowledge of the school language. If the child, on the other hand, attends a minority language programme, it is important that this language be the dominant language, while at the same time maintaining skills in the majority language so that the child will not feel like a foreigner living in the majority language country. Another reason for maintaining skills in the majority language is that at some point in the child's education (unless it returns to the minority language country) it will probably have to switch to instruction carried out in the majority language. (Nevertheless, some parents may choose a minority language programme, especially at the pre-school level, in order to support the child's language development in the minority language.)

2. *Don't leave the task of raising the child
   bilingually to the pre-school or school*

   Even in cases where the child attends a minority language programme at school, parents should still realize that they are an extremely important source of input in the minority language. Parents should, thus, never neglect their own role in raising their children bilingually. Advice to parents concerning ways of supporting the minority language both in and outside the home will be given in the next two chapters.

3. *Listen to the child*

   In Chapter 5 the child was described as being a highly active individual with a strong inner drive to learn to understand, handle, and control its environment. In connection with bilingualism, like adults, children are likely to develop a motivation for using two languages in their environment when they see a purpose for this. The child's motivation may, likewise, shift as conditions in the environment shift with regard to the need for communicating in each of the languages. In addition to developing overall goals for raising the child bilingually, it is important that parents are sensitive to the messages received from the child, while at the same time making an active attempt to introduce factors in the environment which are likely to increase the child's own motivation to want to use and continue to learn each of the two languages.

PART IV:
Practical suggestions

9 Practical suggestions for raising children bilingually inside the home

As was mentioned in Chapter 1, for most immigrant children parents are the main source of input in the minority language. It is thus especially important for immigrant parents that they recognize the important role they play in their children's language development. This chapter will explore ways in which parents can help to enhance their children's language development in the home. The information presented is intended mainly for immigrant and minority group parents, but much of it is also applicable to the majority language parent (i.e. in the mixed-language family setting). Although a number of suggestions are given, it is also realized that fewer and fewer parents are full-time parents these days. Thus, parents should feel free to choose among the various suggestions, finding an activity level which is commensurate with their own time schedule. But parents should realize that, after all, the single most important factor in the child's language development is participating in conversations with interested and supportive communication partners. Thus, this area is considered first in the text. A second area which has been found to be important in raising children bilingually is reading to the child. Parents having little time should, thus, focus on these two areas, which will go a long way towards helping their child achieve bilingual proficiency.

Conversing with children

Parents should never forget that they are experts at the language which the child is learning and, thus, have a great deal to offer the young child. As was mentioned earlier, one of the main ways in which children learn language is during the course of ordinary conversations with parents, siblings and other persons important to the child. Here are some general guidelines for parents which may be useful when conversing with young children.

Two important factors in conversing with children

Ronald Macaulay (1980) in his short but comprehensive book on children's language development suggests that conversations with children will be greatly enhanced if parents follow this following basic principle:

Treat the child as someone whose opinion is valued and whose feelings are respected.

If this advice is followed, two things will automatically happen which are important for language development. Firstly, parents will pay attention to the child and try to understand him/her. An interested listener is, after all, probably the most important factor in language development. Secondly, parents will speak clearly to the child and adapt their speech to the child's level of understanding, so as not to make the child feel ignorant or stupid. This is important because, in order for children to make use of adult input in their own construction of language, this input must match the child's level of development.

A second principle mentioned which is important to keep in mind is that most people find it easier to talk when they feel relaxed and comfortable in their surroundings. Thus, the presence of a loving and accepting environment in which conversation takes place cannot be over-emphasized. Show your acceptance of the child by having an interest and an excitement over what he/she has to say, being enthusiastic over his/her progress, and, quite simply, by spending time with the child.

When to begin conversing with the child

It is safe to say that it is never too early to begin conversing with the child. Many parents state that they feel silly speaking to their infants because the baby "doesn't understand". This feeling is often augmented in situations where the minority-language-speaking parent feels uncomfortable about speaking the minority language to the child in the first place, e.g. in front of relatives who may be critical toward the parents raising the child bilingually.

However, the idea that young children do not benefit from hearing language until they themselves can produce it is incorrect in several ways.

Firstly, through verbally interacting with their parents during routines like dressing, eating, diapering, etc. infants learn a great deal about participating in conversations although they may not yet understand in detail the individual words or phrases being used. Although adults initially take most of the responsibility for these conversations, the infants also play an essential role, learning to take over more and more of the functions formerly performed by the adult as they grow older. An important rule to follow is, thus, to speak to the baby as if it understood what you were saying, speaking clearly and in whole sentences. As children grow older, a second reason for providing as much language input as possible is because children's ability to understand language far exceeds their ability to produce it. Thus, through hearing language spoken around them all the time, children are actively building up knowledge which will later be used in their own productions.

How to converse with young children

In general, parents may, of course, converse in any number of ways with their young children, and each parent will want to explore the types of communication strategies which are most effective with just their particular child. As a general rule, parents should be responsive to the child. If what they are doing seems to be making the child unhappy or to be reducing language production then something is probably wrong with the method.

Learn to make use of the many natural situations in which the child is engaged or in which you and the child are carrying out activities together as a source of conversational exchange. Draw the child into conversation by questioning him about what he is doing, trying not to drown the child in words but asking naturally curious questions which encourage the child to enter a dialogue situation in which there is an active give and take by both partners. This means that parents must learn to be good listeners as well as speakers, allowing the child ample time to express its feelings and thoughts. Conversing with the child should, thus, always be seen as an *exchange* and not consist of a one-sided telling the child what to do or correcting the child.

As was mentioned at the end of Chapter 5, a strategy which has been found to enhance children's language development is the use of simple expansions of the child's own utterances. Expand on what the child says as in the following example. If the child says "doggie", parents might say, "Yes, that's a dog, isn't it?" and then perhaps further question the child about what the dog is doing, etc. This will both show the child one's interest as well as introduce the child to new grammatical structures. When questioning the child, try to avoid yes/no questions which give the child little opportunity to explore ideas and express thoughts, instead asking "What", "Why", "How", and "In what way" type questions. For the child who is particularly shy about using the minority language, parents can help by giving the child "alternate responses", e.g. "Do you want cornflakes or oatmeal for breakfast?" In addition to questioning the child, try and talk as much as possible to the child about what you are doing, discussing with the child, explaining words, and describing objects in the environment. Use language in different ways, e.g. to label, identify, compare, and evaluate, in this way exposing the child to some of the various functions for which language can be used.

Learning is often most effective when the child itself is interested in a particular topic and initiates a conversation about this with the parent. Try to make yourself available to the child at these times rather than waiting until perhaps *you* feel like talking but the child is completely uninterested. As was mentioned in Chapter 5, it is also of course important to recognize that children need time on their own in order to explore the world and analyse and understand their experiences. Thus, although conversing with the child is important, it should not replace other important needs which both parents and children have.

Conversational topics

As the primary purpose of language is the exchange of meaning, this means that any topic which allows parents and children to communicate with one another is useful. It is, thus, not necessary to purchase special games or toys in order to "have something to talk about", although such activities are also useful at times because they may contribute toward making it "fun" or "special" to speak the minority language. In general, parents should instead use the many daily activities which they engage in with their children, such as eating, bathing, dressing, baking, houshold chores, going to the park, doing errands, etc. as a basis for conversational exchange. One reason why such activities are particularly useful is that they are anchored in the here and now. In this way the child can use context to help him/her understand language which is a little beyond the present stage of development, in this way making progress in language development (see Krashen, 1981). Furthermore, such topics are familiar to the child, and it is easier to talk about familiar subjects than new ones. Just because these topics are familiar, however, does not mean that parents cannot gradually bring in new words and concepts in connection with them.

As an example of how one can use everyday activities for language learning, let us take baking. When baking, let the child help, and exchange information about what you are doing together the whole time. For example: "First we must sift the flour (showing the child what "sift" means). Then we add a cup of sugar and mix it together", etc. Use words naturally associated with the activity, especially repeating those which are appropriate for the child's developmental level and encourage the child to actively use these words. Learning language in this way is not only useful because it introduces the child to new words and concepts in the context of a positive emotional atmosphere (i.e. while sharing an enjoyable activity with the parents), but also because it occurs "while doing" which has been found to have a positive effect on learning. Parents should, naturally, also try to converse about activities which *they* enjoy. Conversing about topics which one does not find particularly interesting is likely to put a strain on the conversation which will eventually be perceived by the child.

One activity which seems to be especially useful in encouraging children to use the minority language is role-play. Role-play can be used starting when the child is between two and three years of age. Even children who do not regularly speak the minority language to their parents may be encouraged to do so when taking the role of, for example, puppets who only "speak" the minority language, playing "hospital", "store", or "school", or conversing on a toy telephone with relatives in the minority language country.

One parent also suggests that he has had success in encouraging his young child to use the minority language by using ritualized "naming games" in which the child is only required to "fill in the blank". For example, when naming parts of the body, the parent may point to various body parts, saying, "This is your . . . . and this is your . . . .", etc.

Children need lots of repetition

Children need to hear words and expressions many times before they are able to use them automatically, i.e. without having to reflect on them. This is especially true for the child speaking a minority language, for whom exposure to the language is limited. Therefore, activities in which the child is exposed to new words or phrases need to be repeated frequently. The learning of new words and concepts will also be enhanced if this involves a "total learning experience" in which several senses are involved simultaneously. For example, in learning the word "pillow", rather than just exposing the child to the word while looking at a picture in a book, give the child a real pillow to hold and squeeze while listening to the word. It is also useful to use the same word in a variety of contexts so that the concepts behind the words become clearer to the child. For example, if introducing the word "dog" to the child, parents might expose the child to the child's own dog, dogs on the playground, pictures of dogs in books, dogs on television, etc.

Reading to the child

Parents who are successful in raising their children bilingually seem to read frequently to their children in the minority language, often once per day. Reading to children is important for a number of reasons, not only those having to do with language development:

1. Reading is an activity which offers close emotional contact between parent and child. This is not only important in itself, but also because learning which takes place in such circumstances is facilitated.
2. The child learns from an early age that books are important. This is greatly important for the child's later progress at school where the main way of gaining knowledge about the world is through extracting information from printed materials.
3. Reading increases the child's vocabulary and exposes the child to new language structures.
4. Reading introduces the child to new concepts.
5. Reading increases the child's fantasy.
6. Reading, by offering the child an opportunity to identify with others, helps the child to understand his/her feelings.

When reading to the child, parents should select books which are at the child's level of comprehension or slightly above. For two- to three-year-olds books should contain more pictures than words and these should be large and clear. Young children seem to especially enjoy pictures of animals and people.

According to some experts, a mistake which parents often make when reading to two- and three-year-old children is insisting on reading the text word for word. A better approach is to look at the picture and talk to the child about it, asking the child questions and making sure to give the child ample time to answer. Even more important is taking the time to answer the child's own spontaneous comments on, and questions concerning, the pictures. Just reading the words does not help the child in learning their meaning or how the words and pictures are related. Eventually, however, parents can help the child to associate the words and pictures. It should also be remembered that young children are not able to concentrate for long periods of time. Parents should, thus, only read to the child as long as it remains interested. From the beginning, parents should attempt to make books and reading a pleasurable experience, one which will follow the child throughout its life.

For the older child, stories may be read directly, although always allowing time for questions and discussion. Children may also enjoy making their own books which can be continually added to. These books can be about the child, things he likes to do, the people he knows, etc. A few words of text can be written to accompany each picture.

As the child grows older he/she can also dictate his /her own stories and poems which parents can write down and read back. Children seem to enjoy having parents write down what they say and hearing it read back to them. Parents can also engage in story-telling without books. Most children love hearing stories, for example, about when parents or grandparents were young. Such activities can also be useful in exposing the child to the minority language culture. Or as an alternative, parents and children can take turns in developing a story together.

Parents should also make contact with their local library where librarians can help in suggesting suitable children's books or in obtaining books in the minority language. If the number of immigrant and minority group children from one language background is large enough, it may also be possible for minority language story hours to be organized by the library.

Singing, nursery rhymes and games

Other ways of stimulating the use of the minority language are through singing, nursery rhymes and games. Many parents find that their children greatly enjoy learning songs and nursery rhymes, even when they seem reluctant to use the minority language in ordinary conversations. Singing or chanting words to rhythm also seems to be an aid to memory. Such activities can be used for practising pronunciation, for example, by choosing songs which include sounds which are difficult to pronounce in the minority language. Songs and nursery rhymes are also useful because they often introduce unusual words which can then be explained to the child. For example in the following nursery rhyme:

Jack and Jill
Went up the hill
To fetch a pail of water
Jack fell down
And broke his crown
And Jill came tumbling after,

the word "crown" can be explained to the child, telling the child that it means the same thing as "head". The child can then try substituting the word "head" in the rhyme, seeing what happens, in this way also being introduced to the concept of poetry.

When teaching the child songs or nursery rhymes, remember again that these need to be repeated many times before they are learned. For parents who feel that they are unmusical, and thus may feel self-conscious about singing to the child (although there is no reason why this need be so), the words of the song can be chanted to hand clapping, etc.

Games involving various aspects of language (e.g. word games or those involving practice with letters) can also be used with the older child. Many ideas for games with language are presented in various guidebooks to language learning written for monolingual parents (see Suggestions for Further Reading). Games make learning fun and relaxing, thereby enhancing it, and are useful for both practising what is already known and for motivating the child to learn something new.

Teaching the child to read

According to some experts on early child bilingualism, such as the American, Theodore Andersson, an excellent way to encourage the use of the minority language is by teaching the child to read in this language. Dr. Andersson has written a number of books and articles on this subject, including "A Guide to Family Reading in Two Languages: The Preschool Years" (1981). By teaching the child to read, one can help to compensate for the lack of input in the minority language in the surrounding environment.

Many parents reading this book may be surprised at the suggestion that young children can learn to read. At approximately the age of three, however, many parents notice that their children begin to show an interest in print, which they see all around them, for example, in books, signs, on cereal packages, in the newspapers which they see their parents reading, etc. Special methods have been developed for teaching young children how to read, in order to take advantage of children's apparently natural curiosity at this age. Glenn Doman has published a book called "How to Teach Your Baby to Read" (1975), which has become known as the "Doman method". Many parents have found this method successful or have developed their own methods for teaching their children to read. No matter what method is used, however, it is important not to force the child but to only introduce reading when the child itself is interested.

Some parents may object to the idea of teaching the young child to read as they feel that it is "pushing" the child. Early reading is not intended to pressure the child, however, but, rather, to take advantage of the child's natural interest in learning to understand and control its environment (see Chapter 5), including the printed word. Thus, reading is seen as a rewarding and pleasurable experience for the child and one which can expose the child to new areas of learning. This is supported by the great delight and pride which many children spontaneously show when they are able to decipher a printed message.

Involving the mass media in minority language learning

The exposure to the minority language can be increased by, in addition to books, exposing the child to cassette tapes and children's records with songs and stories, video and television programmes, children's films, children's concerts and plays in the minority language when these are available, etc. Some researchers also point out that the status of the minority language is raised in the child's eyes when it is used in the mass media.

The use of video presents exciting possibilities for the development of the minority language, and many parents have found that video children's programmes are a highly effective way of increasing the child's motivation to use this language. Such films must of course be chosen with discretion, however. Although a valuable accompaniment to the active use of the language, e.g. in conversations, video and television programmes cannot replace the important role which interaction with adults and other children plays. Television and video programmes in the minority language, for example, give the child little training in learning to communicate because the child assumes a passive role. Furthermore, with regard to intellectual development, children need "hands on" experience in addition to visual presentation of information. Nevertheless, if used in the right way, video has many advantages and has been shown to increase children's interest in learning the minority language.

If cassette tapes or children's records are difficult to obtain in the minority language, parents might consider making their own tapes for their children. Short sequences of stories can be recorded as well as songs and nursery rhymes. By teaching the child to operate the tape recorder, parents can provide many hours of enjoyment for their children and provide the child with the opportunity to listen to the minority language when the child itself is interested. Grandparents may also be enlisted in this area. For example, one mother stated that her child's grandparents in the minority language country regularly send 10-minute tapes to the child (purchased at the post office) containing songs, stories, and special messages. These tapes are, needless to say, a great source of enjoyment to the child. They can also give grandparents living in another country a feeling of involvement in the child's development as well as help to allay fears that the child will not be able to communicate in the grandparents' language.

Obtaining ideas from other parents

I frequently meet bilingual families while lecturing, in the context of various immigrant organizations, etc. and find that each family has something new to offer concerning successful methods for raising children bilingually. Thus, it is very useful for parents to "compare notes" whenever possible. Also, many immigrant clubs have special committees or interest groups concerned with issues related to children's bilingualism, from whom valuable tips and suggestions can be obtained. The child's pre-school teacher may also be a source of information concerning ways of stimulating the child's language development in the home.

Additional sources of information are the many practical guidebooks written for monolingual parents concerning ways of stimulating the child's language development, starting pre-school play-groups, etc. A number of these are listed in Suggestions for Further Reading, but parents should also check their libraries and bookstores for additional suggestions. Such books obtained in the minority language country may be especially useful in suggesting activities specifically related to the minority language and culture.

Finally, parents should not be afraid to "let their imaginations loose". The various suggestions in this chapter are only a beginning; parents will undoubtedly be able to think of additional ideas which are suited just to their particular child.

In summary, here are the ideas which have been suggested for stimulating the child's use of the minority language inside the home. In the following chapter we will look at some ways of supporting the minority language outside the home. Before concluding this chapter, however, I would like to briefly mention some problems which are frequently encountered by parents raising their children bilingually in the context of the home.

IDEA BANK

- singing, nursery rhymes and games;
- role-play activities;
- reading to the child;
- borrowing library books in the minority language;
- subscribing to children's magazines in the minority language country;
- storytelling;
- teaching the child to read in the minority language;
- cassette tapes from relatives;
- commercially available cassette tapes and children's records in the minority language;
- video films and television programmes as well as other mass media activities;
- storybook-cassette sets available in some minority languages in local bookstores;

- carrying out activities together which require following written instructions;
- writing letters, poems, and stories.

Some problems which can occur and suggestions for dealing with them

As has been emphasized many times throughout this book, raising children bilingually is, unfortunately, not free of problems. The chapter will conclude with a discussion of possible ways of dealing with some problems frequently mentioned by parents, including the following:

- the child's refusal to speak the minority language;
- older siblings speaking the majority language to the child;
- correction of the child's errors;
- others expressing negative attitudes towards the parents raising the child bilingually.

The child refusing to speak the minority language to the parent

This problem has been mentioned earlier in the text and, thus, will only be considered briefly here. As was mentioned previously, it is highly important that parents maintain a consistent attitude and continue speaking to the child in the minority language under these circumstances. Activities which have been found useful in breaking the pattern of the child's refusal to use the minority language are visits to the minority language country (or other countries in which the minority language is used) or from relatives who do not understand the majority language. Parents also need to accept the fact that there may be some periods in the child's life when the language of the school and peer group assumes priority (e.g. when starting school). By maintaining a patient and tolerant attitude (while at the same time continuing to use the minority language when addressing the child) parents may find that these periods pass and that a balance in the use of the two languages is later resumed.

Thus, it is essential that parents develop a flexible attitude and a long-range outlook with regard to their children's bilingual development.

Older siblings speaking the majority language to the child

Another frenquently mentioned problem is that older siblings speak the majority language to the child, thus greatly reducing the amount of exposure to the minority language which the child receives. It is difficult to solve this problem short of trying to generally increase the use of the minority language among the older children, for example, through spending time in the minority language country. More time can also be spent in family activities during which all family members speak the minority language together, or the minority-language-speaking parent may try to spend more time alone with the child. Parents may, of course, try to explain to older children the importance of their speaking the minority language to the child, but this often has not been found to have a very long-lasting effect.

Correcting the child's errors

When correcting the child it is important to remember that the main purpose of language is communication. Correcting the child should, thus, never hinder the child's communication as this can have a negative effect on the child's willingness to use the minority language altogether. Instead of interrupting the child, a better practice, and one used by many parents, is to repeat the correct form when responding to the child, which the child may then spontaneously imitate.

Parents can also take notes of the errors which the child makes in order to, at some later point, make up exercises or games in which the child can be given training in practising the correct form. Parents should concentrate on several errors at a time until the correct forms are mastered in order not to discourage the child. Direct corrections, as well as explaining the differences between structures in the two languages, can be used with the older child, but this should be done with discretion.

Parents also need to recognize that it will be meaningless to correct some errors because these are simply beyond the child's level of understanding. In other words, language develops systematically and error correction must "match" the child's developmental level in order for it to be effective.

Dealing with negative attitudes by others towards the parent/parents raising the child bilingually

Although many parents raising their children bilingually are fortunate in receiving support from relatives and friends for their efforts, in other cases parents may encounter negative attitudes from others. Such attitudes are of course discouraging, but parents can learn to deal with them by understanding them. In many cases majority language grandparents may be critical towards parents speaking the minority language to the child because they fear that the child will not learn the majority language properly or be able to communicate with them in this language. Such negative attitudes often disappear, however, when it is seen that the child's language development appears to be progressing normally in the majority language. Parents should also try to explain to others what is known about early childhood bilingualism, e.g. the importance of parents speaking their own language to the child in order to be able to communicate naturally and spontaneously with the child, the fact that research findings have not indicated that early bilingualism has negative effects on the child's development or leads to an incomplete mastery of the majority language, etc.

10 Practical suggestions for raising children bilingually outside the home

In addition to using the minority language as much as possible inside the home, the child's motivation will be greatly increased if it has the opportunity to meet other children and adults who speak the minority language outside the home. Arranging for children to participate in minority language activities outside the home also communicates to children the message that parents feel it is important for the child to learn the minority language. Activities outside the home are not only important for exposing the child to the minority language, but to the minority culture as well.

This chapter thus focuses on ways of stimulating the child's use of the minority language outside the home. As was mentioned in Chapter 9, not all parents have a great deal of time to devote to their children's bilingual upbringing. If parents do have limited time, it is important to realize that the single most important factor in raising children bilingually (with regard to factors outside the home) is probably visits to the minority language country. Thus, if parents have minimal time, it is important that they attempt to make these visits as effective as possible. Ways of doing this as well as alternative solutions when parents are unable to visit the minority language country will be discussed later in the chapter.

Compensating for the lack of exposure to the minority language in the child's environment

Unlike the majority language child who has many opportunities for learning his/her mother tongue, e.g. from parents and siblings, relatives, school, playmates, recreational and religious activities, the mass media, etc. for many immigrant and minority group children the exposure to the minority language is limited to the domain of the family. This places a great deal of responsibility on parents who must try to compensate for the lack of exposure to the minority language which would have been provided naturally had the child grown up in the minority language country. Thus, parents should try to expose the child to as many domains of language use outside the family as possible, so that new vocabulary and ways of using the minority language will be developed. For example, take the child with you to the supermarket, drugstore, post office, sports activities, to the country, etc. explaining new words and concepts in connection with these activities. Although it will, of course, not be possible to give the child the wide exposure to the minority language which would have been possible in the minority language country, it will still, in this way, receive greater exposure to the language than if the minority language is restricted to the home domain alone.

Getting together with other families

Try to meet with other families having a similar language and cultural background, as often as possible, for informal get-togethers, outings, special "minority language days", celebrating holidays, etc. This will have a stimulating effect on the child (as well as parents) as the child will learn that it is not only the parents who speak the minority language but others as well. Include families with other children, especially those who are slightly older whom the child can model. Structure these get-togethers somewhat, so that the children will not be left to themselves the entire time which may result in their speaking the majority language to each other.

Play-groups

It is extremely important that immigrant and minority group children have the opportunity to meet other children who speak the minority language as well as share their cultural background. In addition to providing language input this gives the child a group to identify with so that it does not feel "different" from other children due to its being bilingual. It also increases motivation due to the important influence of the peer group. This is especially important for children who do not have the opportunity to visit the minority language country frequently, or participate in bilingual education programmes, etc.

Play-groups in which mothers and toddlers get together once or several times a week are an excellent way of introducing young children to other minority language speakers. These may be organized in a number of ways. In England and Wales there are national organizations to promote the starting of pre-school play-groups and parents may wish to investigate the possibility of carrying out such groups in the minority language. (This is, in fact, being done in Wales.) Play-groups may also be organized by local authorities, through the church, through immigrant organizations or simply by parents getting together in one another's homes.

Some experiences from minority language play-groups

Several years ago I carried out a small research study of minority language play-groups for pre-school children (see Arnberg, 1984). Some experiences from these groups may be of interest to parents wishing to start similar groups and will, thus, be described briefly.

The play-groups were organized in connection with the local municipality which, in Sweden, provides minority language lessons for pre-school children from the age of four years onwards for approximately four hours per week. Both children enrolled in the local day-care programme as well as children cared for in the home by parents are eligible for this programme. A mother/ toddler group for one- to three-year-olds was thus formed in conjunction with the regular minority language programme for four- to six-year-olds. Two leaders were available, who received a small remuneration from the local municipality, but the mothers were expected to actively participate in all phases of the programme.

The children met once per week for approximately three hours. Traditional activities were used with an emphasis on activities promoting language use such as singing, story-telling, dramatics, role-play and working around themes. An attempt was also made to represent the different cultures of the children (e.g. English, Irish, American) in the various activities.

Although the experiences from the group were positive, they did not lead to a dramatic improvement in the minority language; however, this can hardly be expected considering the fact that the group only met once per week. (The effects of the group are, of course, also related to the extent to which the minority language is used in the home.) Nevertheless, the group had an important supportive function for parents in their attempts to raise their children bilingually, led to children developing a more positive attitude towards their bilingualism, and seemed to encourage children to use the minority language outside the group to a greater extent than was the case prior to the group's starting.

Experiences from the group have led to the following suggestions, which may be of interest to parents starting groups in the future:

- with regard to parent involvement, it is important to have a group leader responsible for keeping the group going. However, if parents are to be actively involved in the programme, this should be made clear by leaders from the start. An alternative is to rotate the leadership function among parents;
- it is important to use activities which make it absolutely necessary for the children to actively use the minority language when interacting with others. Thus, long periods spent on activities such as drawing, hand-crafts or other "silent" activities are less fruitful with regard to language development because they often do not result in a great deal of verbalization. (Of course, how language-oriented the activities are, also depends on how frequently the group meets.);
- the children's time needs to be structured as much as possible so that they are not left on their own for long periods during which many children begin to speak the majority language with one another;
- books, songs, etc. need to be geared to the children's developmental level in order for children to remain concentrated and to benefit from them. Due to the children's limited exposure to the minority language this may mean that books for younger children may be more appropriate than books geared to the actual chronological ages of the children. This introduces the problem, however, of finding books whose content is of interest to the child;
- songs and nursery rhymes need to be repeated frequently in order for learning to occur;
- it is desirable to divide the children into a younger (e.g. one- to three-year-olds) and an older (e.g. four- to six-year-olds) group, at least for part of the time, if the age range represented is wide. However, when forming age groups consideration also needs to be taken of the child's maturity, skill in the minority language, etc.;
- it is highly desirable that group leaders be given training concerning ways of supporting children's language development in the minority language if the group is to have a pronounced linguistic effect;
- it is useful to have a schedule which is followed for each meeting in which the individual songs, themes, etc. are interchanged. This provides a continuity to the programme and increases the children's sense of security. A possible schedule for younger children is suggested below by Ann Ahlgren, one of the group mothers.

ACTIVITY PLAN FOR YOUNGER GROUP
(One- to three-year-olds)

Purpose: To become acquainted with the English language through play

1.   Planned free play (20 min.)
      Ex. dolls, cars, dolls' teaset

      Adults talk to children either one-to-one or in groups

2.   Active play (20 min.)
      Ex. singing games, ordinary games, gymnastics, mime and drama

3.   Talking about a topic with pictures (15 min.)
      Ex. animals, traffic, farm, holidays

4.   Eating and drinking (15 min.)

5.   Songs and finger plays (10 min.)

6.   Art activity, optimally related to topic in No. 3 (20 min.)
      Ex. Drawing, modelling clay, etc.

7.   Story (20 min.)
      Ex. Telling a story with flannel board, puppets, or regular story

Activities in immigrant organizations

It is stimulating for immigrant and minority group children to participate in special activities with other children and adults sharing a similar language and cultural background. Many immigrant organizations and clubs sponsor activities for families and children in order to help maintain the minority language and culture. The following are some examples of activities which are provided in the immigrant organization to which I belong, but parents will undoubtedly be able to suggest additional activities which are used in their own particular groups:

- celebrating holidays together;
- family activities such as sports days, picnics, etc.;
- Saturday workshops for children, e.g. in dramatics, dance, baking, ceramics, etc.;
- puppet shows, films, etc.;

- playgroups for mothers and toddlers;
- summer camp programmes.

Through their immigrant organizations, parents can also pool materials so that libraries for exchanging books, video films, children's records, etc. in the minority language can be built up.

Trips to the minority language country

Of all the "methods" for raising children bilingually, as was mentioned in the beginning of the chapter, trips to the minority language country are by far the most important. Extended visits from relatives who do not speak the majority language are also, of course, important. Nevertheless, visits to the minority language country with the opportunity they provide of seeing the minority language and culture in its native context, meeting minority language relatives, etc. seems to have an enormous impact on children. It is, of course, recognized that not all families are able to visit the minority language country. In this case the next best alternative is to visit other countries in which the minority language is used, if possible. Another alternative is special activities provided a prolonged input in the minority language such as summer camp programmes (held in the majority language country). Such a programme is described in greater detail below. The following are some suggestions for utilizing visits to the minority language country as effectively as possible.

With regard to the frequency of the trips, parents should, of course, try to visit the minority language country as often as possible. The ideal would be for such visits to occur once per year. If the family is unable to travel frequently to the minority language country, it is better, from a language point of view, to postpone the visits until the child is at least two to three years of age. By this time the child has begun to recognize the existence of the two languages in the environment and to understand its bilingualism. Although younger children will, of course, also benefit from the exposure to the minority language, it is felt that the older child will be better able to use the time spent in the minority language country.

Try to prepare the child for the trip beforehand, explaining that during the visit everyone will speak like mummy or daddy, and that others will not be able to understand the child if it speaks the majority language. Describe to the child what it will be like in the minority language country, about the people it will meet, and about what sorts of things it will be doing there.

It is a good investment of both time and money, especially if such visits occur infrequently, if the visits last as long as possible, preferably for at least a month, but optimally longer. This is because it may take the child time to adjust to using the minority language on a regular basis.

One thing which has been found to be extremely important in connection with such visits is the child's opportunity to meet other children. Try to find out beforehand if playmates will be available in the child's age range or ask relatives to look into the possibility of children's activities. One mother achieved highly positive results by placing the child in a summer day camp programme for several hours each day, not immediately upon arrival in the minority language country, but shortly thereafter. In connection with this activity the child made rapid progress in the minority language. Other children seem to more strongly motivate the child to speak the minority language than adults, who often adapt to the child's use of the "wrong" language, e.g. by using non-verbal communication, guessing what the child means, etc.

Upon returning home do not be surprised if the child temporarily seems to have "forgotten" the majority language. Many parents report that at first many children speak the minority language to everyone for several days, including majority language playmates (this causing a great deal of confusion!) and does not seem to realize that it is speaking the minority language to others. The ability to directly switch to the majority language upon arriving home appears to be more difficult for younger children than older ones, who are often able to develop strategies for dealing with their dual-language situation (for example, one older child referred to his "majority language" and his "minority language" boxes).

One mother suggests the importance of bringing home reminders of the trip, especially in connection with activities which the child has particularly enjoyed. For example, if the child has enjoyed a certain television programme or film, then toys, games, records, etc. in connection with this activity may be commercially available. Such activities can help the child to later relive the experience of the trip, in this way also helping to stimulate the use of the minority language.

Minority language summer camp

Several years ago I had the fascinating experience of participating in a summer camp programme in Sweden for bilingual English-Swedish-speaking children. I am convinced that this is an excellent way of developing skills in the minority language as well as becoming further acquainted with the minority group culture.

The overnight camp was attended by children for one to two weeks. The children were divided by age groups into a session for older (nine- to

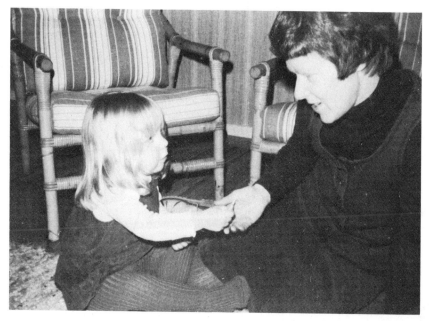

Parents must also be good listeners

Visiting with grandparents in the minority language country: An excellent way of stimulating the development of minority language skills

Getting together with other children in activities sponsored by immigrant organizations

Minority language summer camp: the opportunity to use the minority language in a variety of situations

fourteen-year-olds) and younger campers (five- to eight-year-olds). One of the most positive aspects of the programme was the wide variety of minority skills represented among the children, ranging from passive skills in the minority language to monolingualism in this language (the latter made possible by English-speaking-children residing temporarily in Sweden). The presence of monolingual speakers together with the "Minority Language Only" rule which was strictly enforced in the camp had an important influence in helping to motivate even children with passive skills in the minority language to use this language as much as possible.

Also extremely positive was the opportunity to use language in a wide variety of communication situations due to the range of activities represented in camp life. These ranged from informal bedtime chats between children while lying in their tents, to listening to adults tell stories by the campfire. Although school programmes in the minority language are, of course, vitally important, I feel that camp programmes, such as the present one, are an important complement to them just because language is used in less restricted communication contexts than is often the case in formal institutions like school. Another important factor which greatly aided learning was the fact that language was used in connection with concrete situations such as preparing food, helping to start the fire, etc. which enabled the children to use context as a clue to understanding.

Language learning also occurred in situations which children found relaxing and enjoyable, such as games, this also serving to enhance learning. All of these factors weighed together thus resulted in children making remarkably rapid progress in the minority language even during a period as short as one week. Nevertheless, this was most apparent with regard to children with only passive skills in the minority language, although even children with more active skills felt that they improved in fluency as a result of the one-week language "immersion". Nevertheless, even if the camp has the greatest impact on "passive bilinguals", this is not insignificant, considering the great number of children in bilingual families growing up with only passive skills in the minority language.

In summary, here are the main ideas which have been suggested in this chapter for ways of stimulating the use of the minority language outside the home.

IDEA BANK

- extending the child's vocabulary by visiting the supermarket, bank, drugstore, etc. and explaining words and concepts in connection with these activities to the child;
- play-groups and open pre-school groups;

- trips to the minority language country;
- extended visits from friends and relatives who do not understand the majority language;
- getting together with other families who share the minority language and culture;
- summer camp programmes;
- scouts;
- Sunday school;
- Saturday activities and children's workshops;
- children's and family activities organized by immigrant organizations.

PART V:
Case studies

11 Meet several bilingual families

In this final section I have asked parents from four bilingual (in one case trilingual) families, as well as one adult who has grown up bilingually, to describe their situations and experiences in connection with raising their children or being raised bilingually. Each of these family descriptions is then followed by some brief comments.

Bilingualism in a Polish-Swedish-speaking family

In the first example I have asked the Polish mother with whom we became acquainted in Chapter 1 to describe her situation now, i.e. three-and-a-half years later. (Her daughter, Anna, is now six years old.) The reader may perhaps recall that in her first letter, Anna's mother was extremely upset because, try as she did to speak Polish to her daughter, Anna responded only in Swedish. At that point Anna's mother even questioned whether she should give up her attempts to raise her daughter bilingually altogether. I responded to her letter by stating that her situation was not unusual and that, no matter what, she should continue speaking Polish to her daughter as consistently as possible. Here is what Anna's mother writes about how her situation has developed:

I can now definitely say that Anna can communicate in Polish, although naturally this is at a much simpler level than in Swedish.

It is extremely difficult for me to raise this level. In order to do so, it would probably be necessary for her to participate in some type of lessons in Polish. (I have tried doing this a little at home, but she seems to be unwilling to concentrate then!)

In other words, Anna can make herself understood in Polish and understands everything in connection with the normal, everyday use of the language. She sometimes lacks the correct vocabulary item and her grammar often resembles the most comical linguistic acrobatics! I must also confess that I do not always correct her in these situations, as I do not wish to interrupt her unnecessarily.

Anna's Polish has its "ups" and "downs". When her grandmother from Poland is visiting, she makes every attempt to make herself understood in Polish and is an eager translator between her grandmother and father. During the months of her grandmother's visits she is also more willing to speak Polish with me.

Then her grandmother leaves and Anna returns to what is most comfortable to her, i.e. speaking Swedish even with me. This language gradually takes over more and more until her speech is entirely in Swedish. At such times I sometimes feel really discouraged and think that, surely, she has forgotten all her Polish. This situation can continue for several months when, suddenly, perhaps in connection with a visit from some Pole, my little Swedish daughter spontaneously, and seemingly effortlessly, communicates with the above person in the "forgotten" language. This seems to occur naturally without her thinking that there is anything strange about it.

It is these occasional incidents which encourage me to keep up my efforts. Sometimes if things feel really strained, however, I "treat" her (and myself) to "speaking a little Swedish" with one another because, by now, I have relaxed a bit more and no longer believe that everything will be lost if I am not 100% consistent all the time. It simply isn't. And besides, I have given up my ambition for my daughter to speak Polish perfectly. I have begun to see now that Polish will always be a second language for her. (Perhaps even a third or a fourth language, who knows?) If we just keep the language alive, however, she will have a firm ground on which to continue developing.

I will close by describing in a little more detail Anna's contact with Polish at the present time (with the exception of her grandmother's visits once a year for approximately two months):

1. I speak Polish to her (not always, but most of the time, especially when we are together).
2. I sing songs to her in Polish. (Although she enjoys this she doesn't try to learn the songs herself.)
3. Sometimes I read children's books to her in Polish (although she often seems to prefer Swedish books).
4. She enjoys listening to tapes of programmes from the Polish Radio's Children's Theatre, although I really wonder how much she actually understands of these.

5. Sometimes, although rather infrequently, we meet other Polish-speaking people.

I also want to add that I am trying to enrol Anna in mother tongue lessons at her day nursery. However, this seems difficult as she is the only Polish child living in our area.

Comments

From a rather pessimistic beginning, Anna's mother's second letter shows that by not giving up, her daughter is now able to communicate in Polish, "although at a simpler level than in Swedish". She is also able to speak the language spontaneously when she is motivated to do so. Anna's bilingualism is a good example of what I referred to in Chapter 8 as "Passive Bilingualism". Although she does not use Polish actively with her mother, the language continues to develop by her hearing it spoken to her. Had Anna's mother given up, it is doubtful that Anna would be able to communicate with her grandmother during her visits to Sweden.

Anna's mother might try to do several things in order to encourage her daughter's use of Polish. Firstly, she might expose her daughter to other children who speak Polish. From the description in the letter, Anna's contact with other Polish-speaking people seems to occur mostly in connection with adults. If this is not possible in connection with visits to Poland, it might be arranged in connection with summer camp programmes, Saturday workshops or other language and cultural activities sponsored by Polish immigrant organizations. Meeting other Polish-speaking children is likely to have a positive effect on Anna's motivation to use Polish, and this group will also provide her with a source of identification in connection with her minority language and cultural background.

Secondly, it is important that the mother try to obtain minority language instruction for her daughter in school, if possible, especially so that Anna can learn to read Polish. Perhaps there are even Saturday school programmes in connection with Polish immigrant organizations. Being able to read the minority language will be an important source of input, given the general lack of exposure to Polish in her environment.

An English-Swedish-speaking family choosing to use only the minority language in the home

Nancy, who comes from the United States, and her husband, Ulf, who is Swedish, have both chosen to speak the minority language, i.e. English, in the home. Here is how Nancy describes the situation in her family:

We have been a Swedish-English bilingual family for almost five years, since the birth of our oldest daughter, Amy. Quite honestly, the experience has only been positive. In fact, we are unable to think of any disadvantages.

Formerly, my husband Ulf (a music teacher) and I (an English teacher) spoke Swedish to each other. Our decision to use only English as our home language was a very deliberate and conscious move that we hoped would ensure our children's speaking both languages fluently.

I feel that so far we are well on our way to achieving that goal and have enjoyed other advantages as well. My husband's English has improved from average schoolbook competency to complete fluency and I no longer feel that I am losing my native language. In addition, I think we have enjoyed an awareness of our children's language development that perhaps other parents miss. When I listen to Amy and her younger sister Melanie (two-and-a-half years old) speaking Swedish, it gives me an insight into their life at their day nursery and the language development in Swedish. I can hear what people say to them and what they are learning. In the same way I follow their language development in English in a way I don't think I would have done otherwise.

We have been active in our attempts to see that the children learn English. We have been pretty consistent in speaking only English together. When someone speaks Swedish, he or she is reminded "English please", and they switch back immediately. Ulf has never felt that it has been any problem speaking a "foreign" language to his children and disagrees with the idea that for emotional reasons one should speak one's native language with one's children. I speak English with the girls even in the presence of Swedes, although this might be considered rude. When playing alone together the children use more Swedish than English. Perhaps one plays in one's native language?

When Amy was small we read a great deal to her in English and she listened a lot to English children's records and tapes. Unfortunately, we haven't read very much to Melanie. Amy spoke first in Swedish. First after a one-week stay alone with her American non-Swedish-speaking grandparents she began to consistently speak English. Melanie, on the other hand, when she began speaking spoke only English. When she started speaking, however, we were on a three-week trip to the United States and I think this was probably influential. At present Melanie mixes both languages freely and Amy speaks both Swedish and English well and doesn't confuse the two. Swedish is, of course, strongest. Amy, unfortunately, dislikes participating in mother tongue lessons at her day nursery, but I feel this is because she thinks she is missing out on other fun activities while she is gone. Also, no one likes to be different. This "being different" will perhaps be more of a problem in the future – maybe, maybe not.

But, so far, it is my opinion that denying a child the gift of a second language would be both tragic and unnecessary.

Comments

This family is a good example of what I referred to in Chapter 8 as "Active Bilingualism". It is clear from the mother's description that the majority language is the children's dominant language. One reason for this is undoubtedly the fact that both children have attended Swedish day-care from an early age. (In the area where the family lives there are few other English-speaking families so that it was not possible to start a day-care group in the minority language.) Nevertheless, the children use English on a daily basis, made possible by the fact that English has been adopted as the family language. The mother also states that the children's English is helped greatly by the long summer vacations (the parents are both teachers) during which the English-speaking grandparents visit for three to four weeks each summer. The family has also made two visits to the United States so that the children have been exposed to English in its "native context".

Nancy stated that her husband did not feel handicapped in communicating with his children when using a second language, i.e. English. However, it should be pointed out that Ulf is highly proficient in English; I found this to be true when I visited the family in connection with their first attempts to raise their children bilingually.

Of course, not all families are able to adopt the minority language as the family language. Both parents are more likely to be bilingual when the minority language is an international language such as Spanish, French, English or German. Nevertheless, if the majority language parent is highly fluent in the minority language outside the home, and if the children have good contact with other Swedish speakers, including adults, this strategy seems to lead to highly positive results.

It is difficult to predict what might have happened had Nancy and Ulf decided to use a one person/one language strategy in raising their children bilingually. Quite possibly the children's skills in English would have been more passive. But, as of yet, there have been no studies comparing the long-range skills in the minority language in passive bilinguals like Anna and active bilinguals like Amy and Melanie.

A single-language
Spanish-speaking family

Juana and her husband are from Chile and moved to Sweden for political reasons. She has lived in Sweden for three years and her husband for seven. Before she moved to Sweden she worked as a key-punch operator in a bank, but is now attending a two-year nursing course. Her husband is an artist. They have two daughters, aged one and eight. The younger daughter is cared for at home by her father while the elder daughter attends second grade in a bilingual class.

Juana writes that at home only Spanish is spoken, even between the children. The family socializes only with Spanish-speaking friends and relatives. Despite these contacts with the minority language, Juana is disappointed with the level of Spanish achieved by her children, due to the dominating influence of Swedish outside the home. Although the bilingual school programme is a big help, in all other activities outside the home Swedish is used. Swedish is even used at times among children who are bilingual in Spanish and Swedish, according to the mother.

As the family plans to return to Chile one day, Juana feels that it is highly important that the children learn Spanish. At the same time, as the stay in Sweden will probably be of long duration, it is also important that they learn Swedish. Thus, both parents feel that a bilingual model in both pre-school and school is to be preferred over a mother tongue model as they feel the latter may result in the children not learning Swedish properly.

Juana's letter also focuses on her own adjustment to Sweden, in connection with which she writes the following:

When a political refugee for the first time moves to Sweden, the first experience is one of freedom. Many new experiences and discoveries occur in connection with one's new life, e.g. in connection with the language, customs and culture. During the first period in the new country everything feels wonderful and new, but gradually the situation becomes more and more difficult as the foreignness of everything sinks in. This can be especially difficult, depending on what time of the year one arrives. In contacts with the authorities one feels helpless and inadequate as one is completely unable to express one's feelings and thoughts in the new language. Unfortunately, one can only swallow these feelings of humiliation. With time, things begin to feel more and more normal, but one's feeling of inadequacy with regard to the language is something one must simply learn to live with.

Comments

It is of interest that even in this case where Spanish is spoken exclusively in the home, where the parents socialize only with other Spanish-speaking friends and relatives, and where the children attend a bilingual programme at school, the mother states that she is disappointed in the level of proficiency achieved in the minority language. What can this be attributed to?

One reason may be that this mother has very high expectations with regard to her children's skills in the minority language, due to the fact that the family plans to return to the minority language country. Thus, it may not be sufficient, with regard to the children's future schooling in the minority language country, that they merely speak the language; rather, native-like skills in reading and writing may be considered equally important. Given a mixed-language family in the same situation, however, the proficiency level achieved here might have been seen in a much more positive light.

Juana also states that even children who are bilingual in Spanish and Swedish, speak Swedish to one another at times. It is difficult to know the cause of this without greater detail, but it may reflect the children's perceptions of Swedish as having higher status than Spanish. This may have resulted in the children speaking a great deal of Swedish even in the context of the bilingual programme at school. School programmes can only be expected to reflect attitudes which are prevalent at other levels of society; they do not change these attitudes. Thus, if bilingualism is not seen in a positive light at the societal level, such attitudes are likely to be reflected in school life. The expression of such attitudes can sometimes be quite subtle, e.g. being reflected in teachers' behaviour, the way the languages are assigned to various subject areas in the classroom, etc. Developing positive attitudes toward bilingualism at the societal level, of course, takes time. This makes it all the more important that parents, in their own behaviour, illustrate the positive aspects of bilingualism and biculturalism.

What, more specifically, can Juana do to encourage the development of minority language skills in her children? One suggestion concerns the role of books and reading in the home, a topic about which nothing is mentioned. Also, Spanish-speaking parents, when getting together with one another, may wish to structure their children's activities to a greater extent, thus encouraging the use of Spanish and illustrating to the children that this language has status and importance. Also important would be offering the children opportunities to meet other Spanish-speaking children who do not speak Swedish. This could be accomplished through minority language summer camp programmes in which "recent arrivals" from Spanish-speaking countries are invited to participate, participation in various children's activities in connection with visits to Spanish-speaking countries, etc. Such activities, of course, cannot replace the benefits of visits to the minority language country and the opportunity to meet grandparents, cousins, etc. but are at least a good substitute, when the option of such visits is rarely open to the political refugee.

Juana's letter also touches on another important point which I recognize from my own adjustment to Sweden, i.e. a tendency to want to socialize only with members of one's own group and perhaps to try and establish "a little United States" or "a little Chile" in the new country. (I remember during my first year in Sweden that I even had nightmares about deserting my country!) Somehow there is the feeling that if one adjusts to the new country, this means giving up one's identity.

During my years as an immigrant, however, I have come to understand that accepting one's new country does not mean that one has to give up the old; in other words, one does not need to choose but can have both. It is also important to realize that Sweden is not a bilingual or even a bicultural country. Thus, building up a wall around oneself amounts to maintaining a false picture of the world, the confrontation with which can be extremely painful. Such confrontations are also inevitable as there will be many times when contact with the majority culture is unavoidable. (Juana's contact with the Swedish authorities illustrates this point.)

Thus, it is extremely important that one becomes open to the new country while at the same time maintaining ties with the old. This is, of course, not easy and as the Swedish writer (of Greek origin), Theodor Kallifatides, has suggested, "To be an immigrant is to be continually tired!" Nevertheless, it is a task which must be carried out by *all* family members. Although this discussion is in no way intended to belittle the highly difficult situation of the political refugee, I nevertheless feel that it is one which applies to all immigrants. As was mentioned in Chapter 2, parents are models for their children's behaviour. Thus, if immigrant and minority group parents do not demonstrate the value of bilingualism and biculturalism in their own behaviour, it is difficult to see how positive attitudes toward these areas will develop in their children.

A trilingual
Finnish-Kurdish-Swedish-speaking family

Helena comes from Finland and moved to Sweden as an adult. Her husband is a Kurd from Turkey who spoke Kurdish in the family and Turkish outside the home. He moved to Sweden after completing high school. In

Sweden he completed studies to become a psychologist. They have a son and a daughter, age six and four. Here is Helena's description of her family's trilingual situation:

It was completely clear from the very beginning that both of us would speak Finnish and Kurdish respectively to our children. We never discussed any other alternative with any seriousness. Both of us felt that this would be the correct and the best thing to do. We have always spoken Swedish with each other.

We have followed our children's linguistic development with great interest. We have never really experienced any "difficult" periods or periods during which the children mixed their languages a great deal, although we were prepared for this. At all times we have tried to be very consistent in speaking our own languages to the children. Both children were about two-and-a-half when they first realized that we (the parents) spoke a different language to each other than we did to them and they found this very amusing. This was when we literally saw how their linguistic awareness opened up in a very positive sense.

This highly positive situation continued until the children were approximately five and two, when their father was forced to move to another part of the country. Since then he has only been able to see the children infrequently. This was a very unfortunate experience and has also meant that the children's Kurdish deteriorated rapidly. It was only a matter of weeks before one began to notice how their vocabulary began to fade away. Within a couple of months they developed a certain resistance toward responding in Kurdish to Kurdish-speaking visitors to the home.

The children's contact with each language in and outside the home

My son was at home with me during his first year. At the end of that year his Finnish and Kurdish vocabularies were nearly equal, although his command of Swedish was minimal. From the age of 1:0 he was cared for by a Swedish-speaking day-care mother. During that year his Swedish vocabulary expanded rapidly; yet, all three languages were somehow equally maintained, each being clearly identified with particular speakers. His sister was born when he was 1:11, and the following year I stayed at home with both children. Although the Finnish input was greater than the Kurdish at this time, the difference was not extremely noticeable. As a family we did not isolate ourselves from the surrounding neighbourhood; thus, the chidren played frequently with Swedish-speaking children. As a consequence, our son quickly developed a good command of Swedish, mainly due to a boy (one year older) in the family next door. His Finnish and Kurdish sounded fluent for his age, although some interference errors were noticed. He experienced no difficulty with pronunciation in Finnish, although some sound replacements were noticed in Kurdish.

When the children were 3:0 and 1:2 respectively they began attending a Swedish day-care centre. We always addressed our children in our own languages even in this Swedish-speaking setting and the children accepted this as natural from the start. (At this point, many parents tend to use Swedish with their children in order not to make the personnel feel uncomfortable.) The input in Swedish was very strong during the year that followed. As parents we tried to provide as much input as possible in each of the languages at home by devoting most of our time to playing, reading and talking with our children. We both did this separately, taking turns, trying to pay equal attention to both children and both languages. At the dinner table we each continued speaking our own languages to the children, switching to Swedish when addressing each other. We felt totally comfortable doing this, although we did have a grasp of what the other parent was saying as the vocabulary is at a rather concrete level when addressing young children. (Although we have both visited both countries, neither of us has studied the other's language systematically.)

Now that the father is living in another part of the country and will probably continue doing so for a further period of time, the children's active languages are Finnish and Swedish. I try to devote as much time as possible to the children when they are at home. Due to my working full time and the long commuting hours, the children's daily stay at their day-care centre is too long, which means greater exposure to Swedish. I have also noticed that the time of year also plays a role. During the winter when it gets dark early, the children more often than at other times play at home. During the light, summer months, however, they want to play outdoors with their friends. I am conscious of these factors and try to compensate for them as much as possible by providing enjoyable activities in Finnish. For example, we shall soon visit my parents in Finland for a month or so, during which time all of the children's social contacts will be in Finnish. This will mean a great deal language-wise. It would also be ideal if we could visit Finland at least three to four times a year at regular intervals. Several months ago a Finnish-speaking boy, aged five, moved in next door. This has been extremely positive for the children's language development in Finnish. The three children speak Finnish with one another, although they switch to Swedish when a Swedish-speaking person joins the group. The children also receive several hours per week training in Finnish at the day-care centre. (Although we discussed a Finnish day-care centre for our children, this was impossible as the closest is approximately 15 kilometres from our home.)

The situation is quite different for Kurdish. The children's only exposure to this language is provided by families who visit us, although this does occur regularly. According to the policy in the community where we live, the children are only allowed to receive lessons in the minority language in one of their minority languages; thus Kurdish is excluded. Even when the children meet other Kurdish-speaking families, however, the children in these families often speak Swedish with one another, which I find very sad. I still talk about Kurdish to the children, about the traditions I know, etc. And the children will always have a Kurdish father. But the long lapse of time without exposure to Kurdish on a daily basis has meant a language change to Swedish for the older child in terms of the language used with the father. (We parents need to handle this situation with care as it is a psychologically delicate one.) Our son still remembers expressions in Kurdish, however, which are highly emotionally coloured. When the children become older we hope that they will be able to visit their Kurdish grandparents for a longer visit, a strong motivation for at least maintaining a positive emotional attitude towards the language.

Have our attempts to raise our children bilingually been successful?

The method of systematically using our own language when addressing our children (i.e. a one person/one language strategy) has turned out to be successful. Up to the ages of five and three for the two children, both children were trilingual. Although they were not equally proficient in all three languages, the differences were quite small. In comprehension, they had nearly an equal command of all three languages. As for their productive ability, Kurdish was somewhat weaker than both Finnish and Swedish. This can be explained by the fact that contacts with Kurdish speakers were fewer than those with Finnish and Swedish speakers. As for Swedish, the children's contacts were mainly with children outside the home. Neither of us "taught" the children Swedish systematically, although we occasionally helped them by letting them know the Swedish equivalents of certain words when this seemed important. During the period age 1:1 to 1:11 for our son, there was certainly a more systematic attempt to "teach" the child certain concepts in Swedish on the part of his Swedish-speaking day-care mother. The next period of systematically learning Swedish was in connection with their attending the Swedish day-care centre (at age 3:0 for the boy and 1:2 for the girl). As was mentioned earlier, their Swedish developed rapidly, soon becoming equivalent to that of the other children at the centre, most of whom were growing up in mixed-language families. (We live in a student apartment building with a strong international atmosphere.) According to the pre-school teachers, however, our children did not differ from Swedish children in terms of vocabulary size, although some errors in word order were noticed.

Our satisfaction with the method used

Both of us were agreed about the language pattern to be used in the family and felt strongly that this would be the best way of successfully raising our children bilingually. We also felt highly motivated in exposing our children to the two languages. We were fully aware of the fact that this would require a lot of extra work. Our conscious devotion to raising our children bilingually means active participation in play, reading, talking, explaining, etc. We have never experienced a lack of willingness to use the languages on the part of the children (i.e. with regard to Finnish and Swedish), and thus contact with relatives in Finland has been most natural. So far, it seems that our children feel competent in speaking Finnish. There are certain transition periods, however, when difficulties are experienced. For example, during certain periods the boy's Finnish has been characterized by an increase in loan-words from Swedish, e.g. when starting the day-care centre at the beginning of the autumn and spring terms. During these times parents must become sensitive to the needs of their children in order not to make them feel inferior in any way when borrowing words, etc.

Advice to other parents in a similar situation

1. Discuss, read about, and become interested in bi/multilingualism.
2. Make a clear decision about the languages to be used in the family *before* the child is born.
3. Do not listen to authorities as experts: many doctors, nurses, relatives, etc. have no, or minimal, knowledge about multilingualism. Instead consult other multilingual families, as many as possible, having their own experiences with this area.
4. Practise your decision about raising your child bilingually the very day your child is born. Talk to the baby even before this so that he/she becomes accustomed to your voice.
5. Continue speaking your language to your child even when speakers are present who do not understand this language; if the message is intended for all, translate it for others.
6. Never give up, feel ashamed, or feel unsuccessful if your child fails to answer you in the language spoken. Do not let the child feel inferior or ashamed either but, in a friendly way, let him/her know the words or expressions in your language.
7. Be aware of the fact that, as a parent, you need to be very active and that you will have to devote much of your time to your child. I still feel that this "requirement" is possible to fulfil without becoming highly unnatural.

8. Join or start a group of interested bi/multilingual families in order to have an informal forum for discussing the process of becoming bi/multilingual – a process with its own ups and downs, just like life itself!

Comments

I am grateful for the care and detail which have gone into this mother's description of her family's trilingual situation, which I am certain will be of interest and help to other families in this situation. Helena's letter shows that it is possible to raise children trilingually, providing that adequate input is available in the three languages in the child's environment. Nevertheless, this does not necessarily mean that all three languages will be perfectly balanced, nor that trilingualism will be maintained if changes with regard to input occur.

It is important to point out that both of these parents appear to be highly motivated in raising their children bilingually, giving this task high priority in family life. Helena feels (as she has stated to me privately) that raising children bilingually is possible in any family, given that the parents are provided with the correct information and are aware of the important role they play in raising their children bilingually. Nevertheless, it is obvious that Helena and her husband have devoted a great deal of time and energy to their children's language development, an effort which not all parents (and children) may be willing to make. Thus, it is important that parents realize that there are other levels of bilingualism which can also be aimed at (for example, "Passive Bilingualism") which, although they may not lead to the same degree of bi/trilingualism which has resulted in Helena's case, may nevertheless lead to a good level of proficiency in the minority language(s).

Another special point about these particular parents is their acceptance of one another's languages, even when they do not fully understand them. (This is in fact a stumbling point for many mixed-language families.) Through showing support and acceptance of their partner's language and a positive attitude toward its being spoken in the home, Helena and her husband demonstrate that it is not absolutely essential for parents to have a full command of the "other" language in order to raise their children bilingually.

Looking back on growing up bilingually

Many parents may be curious to know "what happens" to children who are raised bilingually. The final example thus focuses on an adult who was raised bilingually in the home from early childhood. Markku, age 38, has grown up in Sweden and works as a research associate at the University. Both his parents are from Finland. The eldest of four brothers, he moved to Sweden when he was four. Here is how he describes his situation:

During the first years in Sweden we socialized almost exclusively with other Finnish immigrants. There were, however, many Swedes in the neighbourhood where we lived which meant that I learned Swedish before starting school. At home, however, only Finnish was spoken, even amongst us brothers. Eventually, though, as we learned Swedish, Swedish became the language used between us brothers while Finnish was spoken to our parents. Since this was during the 50's, i.e. before adult education programmes in Swedish as a Second Language became established, it took a long time before my parents could speak more than single words in Swedish.

My mother began a correspondence course in Swedish at about the same time I started school. She also learned Swedish through becoming involved in my schoolwork, checking my homework, etc. As she was a housewife, her main contact with the language (and culture) was through her children. Most of our summer vacations when I grew up were spent either visiting relatives in Finland or receiving visitors from there.

With my parents I have always spoken Finnish and continue to do so to this day. At some point, this began to occur with Swedish words being borrowed when a vocabulary item was lacking in Finnish. Even now many Swedish words appear in the Finnish conversations between my mother and me. These can be easily combined with various prefixes and suffixes in Finnish. My father, on the other hand, has been more consistent about only speaking Finnish, maintaining the language with the help of Finnish newspapers which he reads daily.

My next eldest brother and I began speaking Swedish with each other once he began school and learned the language. I remember that our next youngest brother (four years younger than I) did not speak Swedish in the beginning; thus he was excluded from many of our play activities. My youngest brother, ten years younger than I, is the one who heard the least Finnish at home. Nevertheless, because he spent many summers in Finland where he had cousins in the same age group, he is the one of us who is clearly the most proficient in Finnish. He now works for a Finnish company in Sweden.

During all my school years there was only one term in the second grade during which I had another Finnish-speaking classmate. We spent a lot of time together, spoke Finnish with each other, and sometimes had fights with the other children. (Especially in grade school it was expected that if you were Finnish you could fight!) Otherwise, there were no other Finnish families with children in our neighbourhood after I began school. So my use of Finnish in school was limited to the occasional question from the teacher about the pronunciation of a particular name during geography class. This, of course, was a source of pride for me, i.e. knowing something that the teacher didn't! So my feelings about bilingualism while growing up were both positive and negative.

During certain periods of my childhood I felt it was embarrassing speaking Finnish (e.g. with my parents) in front of Swedes, thereby disclosing my identity. Nevertheless, now as an adult I have definitely felt my Finnish background to be an advantage. I have made good use of my Finnish during a number of business trips and conferences in Finland. I have also done some translations of Finnish technical texts to Swedish, although this is time-consuming due to my lack of familiarity with the written language. What I greatly regret today is that I did not receive any training in reading or writing the language.

How bilingual am I today? Actually I don't feel that my Finnish has really developed or changed substantially since I was nine or ten years old. In addition, it is only a spoken language for me, although naturally spoken without an accent. Nevertheless, I have had more training as an adult (e.g. with regard to vocabulary) than two of my brothers due to the use of the language during visits to Finland in connection with my job. This is important as very little new is learned in connection with everyday conversations in the language, e.g. with relatives. Naturally, my Swedish is native-like due to the fact that I have always attended Swedish schools.

As far as advantages and disadvantages go, I really can't see any disadvantages with bilingualism. I feel that many immigrant children today risk "losing" their mother tongue and thus also losing an important source of contact with their parents. In addition this results in a loss of contact with one's "roots" in terms of earlier generations, relatives in the minority language country, etc.

With regard to my identity, among Swedes I feel like a Swede. In Finland I do not feel like a stranger and feel accepted by Finns, but know that my home is in Sweden. (My heart, however, is in Finland.)

Looking back, I don't really feel that my parents consciously made an effort to raise us bilingually. Their speaking Finnish to us was rather the result of the fact that this was the only language they could easily express themselves in. I remember as a child thinking that my parents couldn't speak Swedish, and therefore there was no point in their trying to speak it to us. If my parents had made more of a conscious decision to raise us bilingually, I believe we would have been exposed more to Finnish books, practised writing the language at home, etc. My personal opinion is that parents should speak the language they know best to their children. Only in this way can they convey their innermost thoughts and feelings to their children.

Comments

This letter describes a rather typical situation in which the parents do not really appear to have made a conscious decision to raise their children bilingually but, rather, in which bilingualism has more or less evolved as a result of natural circumstances. Nevertheless, because the parents continued to lack proficiency in speaking Swedish and because visits to the minority language country occurred regularly, the minority language was maintained. Had the parents been more proficient in Swedish and/or had the family not lived as geographically close to the minority language country as they did, the minority language might well not have been passed on to the children.

Markku's experiences in growing up bilingually appear to have been both positive and negative. On the one hand, he was apparently teased by his classmates for being Finnish. This, as well as his comment about not wanting to disclose his identity in front of Swedes, exemplifies the unfortunately common situation in which one of the bilingual's languages is stigmatized, a situation which many immigrant children are confronted by. On the other hand, his bilingualism was also sometimes a source of pride to him in school, has been a definite advantage to him in his work, and has given him the opportunity of being exposed to another culture, to relatives in the minority language country, etc. Thus, parents might learn from this description that even if bilingualism does occasionally cause difficulties to the child while growing up, this does not mean that it will not be appreciated by the child when he/she is older.

Markku does not feel that bilingualism has negatively influenced his learning of Swedish, although he stated to me that he sometimes wonders if he might have been even better in Swedish had he come from a Swedish-speaking home. He seems to have identified with both of his countries. The main disadvantage with his bilingualism appears to be that he never learned to read and write the minority language. Had he been growing up 20 years later, however, such instruction would most likely have been provided by mother tongue lessons at school (at least in Sweden). However, parents may wish to be aware of the important role they play in imparting such skills to the child when no other source of teaching is available. Being able to read Finnish books would, undoubtedly, also have enabled Markku to develop his minority language skills instead of their being stabilized at age nine or ten.

I was curious as to why Markku seems to have managed so well at school and in his career while many immigrant children in a similar situation experience enormous difficulties. Markku attributes this in part to the fact that he was the only Finnish child in his class and thus was forced to learn Swedish. He states, furthermore, that his parents' rural background was highly similar to that of the families of the other children in his classroom. Thus, one cannot say that he was confronted by a foreign culture in school.

Nevertheless, although it is true that many children do manage this difficult situation, one cannot conclude from this example that placing a child directly in a majority language class is advisable. In Markku's case, he may have, for instance, been a strong and confident child, had especially good teachers, had parents who were highly supportive, etc. It is also important to point out that he was, after all, familiar with Swedish when he started school.

Many children, however, especially those having minimal skills in the majority language, do not manage such a situation well and I believe it is fair to say that it is poorly understood just how difficult this situation probably is for many children. (If this were not the case, there would perhaps be fewer examples throughout the world of this detrimental practice being carried out.) Thus, as has been emphasized at several points throughout this book, it is best to place the minority language child in a minority language classroom initially, at least until the child has made an adjustment to the majority language and culture.

Appendix

Family bilingualism
rating scale

In mixed-language families the following questionnaire should be filled in by the parent speaking the minority language. A point on the 5-grade scale should be circled for each question. This score (from 1 to 5) should then be multiplied by the figure appearing in the answer column and the total sum written in the space provided. Add up the points for all the questions and compare your score with the guidelines below.

Parents should realize that the range of scores appearing below is a rough estimate only. The questionnaire should be seen only as an aid to parents, i.e. one possible source of information in their decision concerning which level of bilingualism they should aim at. Although the scores given are based on a number of actual families, there are always exceptions, and many parents do manage to raise their children bilingually even in circumstances where there is very little support from the outside environment.

Scores of 200 or above: If a score of 200 or above is achieved, experience has often shown that circumstances are very positive for raising the child bilingually. Parents having scores in this range may wish to aim for absolute bilingualism.

Scores of 150 to 199: With regard to scores in this range experience has shown that circumstances are fairly positive for raising the child bilingually. Parents having scores in this category may wish to aim for active bilingualism.

Scores below 150: With regard to scores below 150 experience has shown that it is fairly difficult to raise the child bilingually. Parents having scores in this category may wish to aim for passive bilingualism.

1.   How often does (or will) the mother speak the minority language to the child?

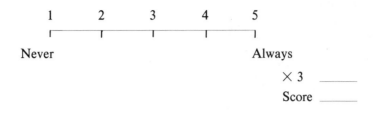

$\times$ 3 _____

Score _____

2.   How often does (or will) the father speak the minority language to the child?

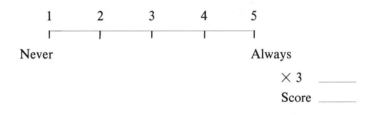

$\times$ 3 _____

Score _____

3.   How often is the minority language spoken between the parents in the home?

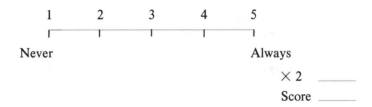

$\times$ 2 _____

Score _____

4.   How often do older sisters and brothers in the family speak the minority language in the home?

$\times$ 3 _____

Score _____

5.   What is the availability of minority language materials for children (e.g. books, records, games, cassette tapes, video films, etc.) in your minority language?

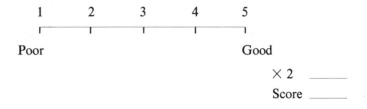

Poor   Good

                                    × 2   _____
                                    Score _____

6.   How difficult do you feel it is to learn other languages yourself? (Combine scores for both parents and divide by two.)

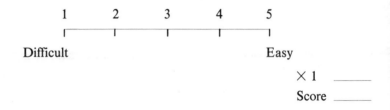

Difficult   Easy

                                    × 1   _____
                                    Score _____

7.   How often does the family visit the minority language country?

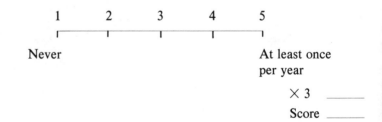

Never   At least once
                                    per year

                                    × 3   _____
                                    Score _____

8.   Does the family plan to return to the minority language country?

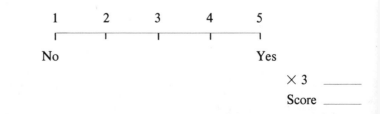

No   Yes

                                    × 3   _____
                                    Score _____

9.   Are there other families from the minority language group living in your neighbourhood?

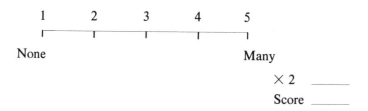

None   Many

× 2   _____

Score _____

10.   How often does the family meet friends and relatives who speak the minority language?

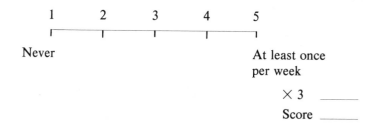

Never   At least once
                                              per week

× 3   _____

Score _____

11.   How active is the family in immigrant/minority group organizations representing the minority language and culture?

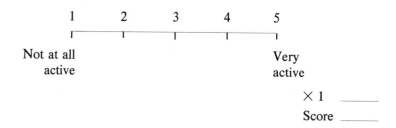

Not at all   Very
active   active

× 1   _____

Score _____

12.   How often does the family attend religious services in the minority language?

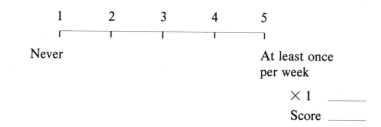

Never   At least once
                                              per week

× 1   _____

Score _____

13. How often does the family participate in cultural activities representing the minority language (e.g. theatre, concerts, listening to radio and television programmes, reading newspapers and magazines, etc.)?

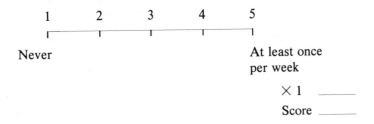

14. How would you judge the attitudes of majority language speakers toward your minority language and cultural group?

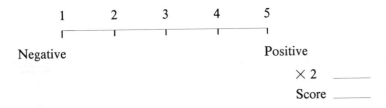

15. How important is it for parents to maintain ties with the minority language and cultural group? (In families where both parents are immigrants/ minority group members, add the scores for both parents together and divide by two.)

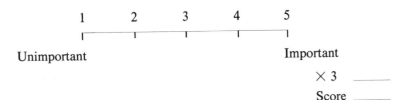

16. Do you expect that the child will attend a pre-school in which the minority language is used?

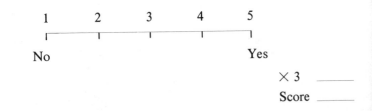

17. Do you expect that the child will attend a school in which the minority language is used?

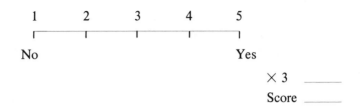

No   Yes

× 3 _____
Score _____

18. Do you feel that the minority language will be useful to the child in its adult life, e.g. in work, education, etc.?

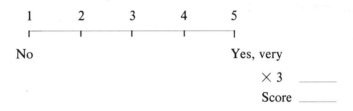

No   Yes, very

× 3 _____
Score _____

19. How important do you feel it is to be able to communicate with the child in the minority language? (In families where both parents are immigrants/ minority group members, add the scores for both parents together and divide by two.)

Not especially   Very
important   important

× 3 _____
Score _____

20. How much time is available for language training in the minority language through the use of games, reading, singing, explaining, etc.?

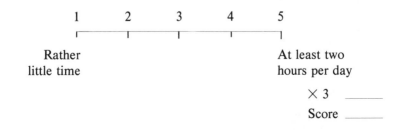

Rather   At least two
little time   hours per day

× 3 _____
Score _____

21. What are your relatives' (from both sides of the family) attitudes toward
raising your child bilingually?

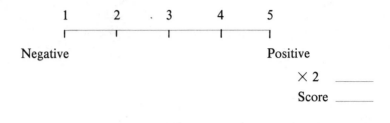

Negative   Positive

                                        × 2   _____
                                        Score _____

Checklist of the Most Important Points Covered in This Book

- Bilingualism is important not only for the individual, but for society as well.
- Parents are models for their children's behaviour; thus, parents' own attitudes towards bilingualism are highly important in shaping their children's attitudes towards their own bilingualism.
- Research findings have not consistently shown bilingualism to have either positive or negative effects on the child's development; however, this does not mean that bilingualism does not result in many advantages for the individual.
- Unless there are stable sources of input in each language outside the home, research findings have shown that great effort will be required of parents in order to achieve a high degree of bilingualism in their children.
- A number of different processes are involved in the child's language learning. These include:
  - reinforcement from others
  - imitation and modelling of others' behaviour
  - certain inborn abilities
  - the child's own inner motivation to steer his/her activities and to understand and structure the world, including language
  - an active interaction with others who are meaningful to the child
- Both simultaneous (learning both languages at the same time) and successive (learning one language after the other) bilingualism during early childhood can lead to a high degree of bilingualism in later years.
- Parents may use different strategies in raising the child bilingually. These include:
  - a mixed strategy
  - a one person : one language strategy
  - speaking only the minority language in the home
  - an initial one-language strategy
- Parents may aim toward different goals with regard to their children's degree of bilingualism, e.g. passive, active and absolute bilingualism. Thus, even parents who are unwilling to exert a great amount of effort may successfully raise their children bilingually by aiming for a passive approach during the early years which, in later life, may result in a more active use of the two languages when the child's own motiviation takes over.
- Children learn various aspects of language more or less easily at various ages; however, there are a number of reasons for exposing the child to both languages at an early age whenever possible.
- Children learn best when they are relaxed and happy; therefore, parents should strive to make language learning as fun as possible for the child.
- Children need to be exposed to the minority language outside the home as much as possible, especially in connection with activities involving other children.
- Although general information can be given, it is the author's opinion that the choice of whether and how to raise the child bilingually can only be made by the individual family because each family knows their own situation best.

References

ANDERSSON, T., 1981, *A Guide to Family Reading in Two Languages: The Preschool Years.* Los Angeles, Ca.: Evaluation, Dissemination and Assessment Center, California State University.

ARNBERG, L., 1979, Language Strategies in Mixed Nationality Families, *Scandinavian Journal of Psychology,* 20, 105–12.

— 1981, *Early Childhood Bilingualism in the Mixed-Lingual Family.* (Doctoral dissertation, Linköping University, Sweden.) University Microfilms International No. 82-70,003.

— 1984, Mother Tongue Play-groups for Pre-school Bilingual Children, *Journal of Multilingual and Multicultural Development,* 5:1, 65–84.

ARNBERG, L. & ARNBERG, P.W., in press, The Relation between Code Differentiation and Language Mixing in Bilingual Three- to Four-Year-Old Children. Accepted for publication in *Bilingual Review.*

BAKER, N.D. & NELSON, K.E., 1984, Recasting and Related Conversational Techniques for Triggering Syntactic Advances by Young Children, *First Language,* 5, 3–22.

BARRETT, M.D., 1982, Distinguishing between prototypes: The early acquisition of the meaning of object names. In S.A. KUCZAJ II (ed.), *Language Development, Volume 1: Syntax and Semantics.* Hillside, N.J.: Lawrence Erlbaum Associates.

BLOOM, L.M., 1970, *Language Development: Form and Function in Emerging Grammars.* Cambridge, Mass.: MIT Press.

— 1973, *One Word at a Time: The Use of Single Word Utterances before Syntax.* The Hague: Mouton.

BOYD, S., 1985, *Language Survival: A Study of Language Contact, Language Shift and Language Choice in Sweden.* Doctoral dissertation, University of Gothenburg, Sweden.

BROWN, R., 1965, *Social Psychology.* New York: Free Press of Glencoe.

— 1973, *A First Language: The Early Stages.* Cambridge, Mass.: Harvard University Press.

CLARK, H.H. & CLARK, E.V., 1977, *Psychology and Language.* New York: Harcourt, Brace & Javanovich.

CONDON, W.S. & SANDER, L.W., 1974, Neonate Movement Is Synchronized with Adult Speech: Interactional Participation and Language Acquisition, *Science,* 183, 99–101.

DE HOUWER, A., 1984, Some Aspects of the Simultaneous Acquisition of Dutch and English by a Three Year Old Child, *Nottingham Linguistic Circular,* December, (Special issue on applied linguistics).

DE VILLIERS, J.G. & DE VILLIERS, P.A., 1978, *Language Acquisition.* Cambridge, Mass.: Harvard University Press.

DOMAN, G., 1975, *How to Teach Your Baby to Read.* Garden City, New York: Doubleday & Co., Inc.

EIMAS, P.D., SIQUELAND, E.R., JUSCZYK, P. & VIGORITO, J., 1971, Speech Perception in Infants, *Science,* 171, 303–306.

GARDELL, I., 1978, *Internationella adoptioner. En rapport från allmäna barnhuset.* Stockholm, Sweden.

GROSJEAN, F., 1982, *Life with Two Languages: An Introduction to Bilingualism.* Cambridge, Mass.: Harvard University Press.

HOFFMAN, C., 1985, Language Acquisition in Two Trilingual Children, *Journal of Multilingual & Multicultural Development,* 6:6, 479–95.

HUANG, J. & HATCH, E., 1978, A Chinese Child's Acquisition of English. In E. HATCH (ed.), *Second Language Acquisition: A Book of Readings.* Rowley, Mass.: Newbury House.

JAKOBSON, R., 1941, *Kindersprache, Aphasie und allgemeine Lautgesetze.* (Språkvetenskapliga Sällskapets i Uppsala Förhandlingar 1940–42). English translation (1968), *Child Language, Aphasia, and Phonological Universals.* The Hague: Mouton.

JENSEN, J.V., 1962, Effects of Childhood Bilingualism. *Elementary English,* 39, 132–43; 358–66.

KJOLSETH, R., 1982, Bilingual Education Programs in the United States: For Assimilation or Pluralism? In P.R. TURNER (ed.), *Bilingualism in the Southwest.* Tucson: The University of Arizona Press.

KRASHEN, S.D., 1981, *Second Language Acquisition and Second Language Learning.* Oxford: Pergamon Press.

LAMBERT, W.E., GILES, H. & PICARD, O., 1975, Language Attitudes in a French-American Community, *Linguistics,* 158, 127–52.

LEOPOLD, W.F., 1954, A Child's Learning of Two Languages, *Georgetown University Monograph Series on Language & Linguistics,* 7, 19–30.

LINELL, P. & JENNISCHE, M., 1980, *Barns uttalsutveckling.* LiberLäromedel Lund.

MACAULAY, R., 1980, *Generally Speaking: How Children Learn Language.* Rowley, Mass.: Newbury House.

McLAUGHLIN, B., 1984, *Second-Language Acquisition in Childhood: Vol. 1. Preschool Children.* (second ed.) Hillsdale, N.J.: Lawrence Erlbaum Associates.

MÉTRAUX, R.W., 1965, A Study of Bilingualism among Children of U.S.–French Parents, *French Review,* 38, 650–65.

NAUCLÉR, K., 1985, *"James Borg, det är en duktig man . . ." Om skillnader i barns samtal med barn och med vuxna.* Göteborgs Universitet, SPRINS-rapport 29.

NELSON, K., 1973, Structure and Strategy in Learning to Talk, *Monogr. Soc. Res. Child Dev.,* 38, No. 149.

OCHS, E. & SCHIEFFELIN, B.B., 1984, Language acquisition and socialization. In R.A. SHWEDER & R.A. LEVINE (eds), *Culture Theory: Essays on Mind, Self and Emotion.* Cambridge: Cambridge University Press.

OLLER, K., 1980, The emergence of the sounds of speech in infancy. In G.H. YENI-KOMSHIAN, J.F. KAVANAGH & C.A. FERGUSON (eds), *Child Phonology, Vol. 1: Production.* New York: Academic Press.

OLLER, K., WIEMAN, L., DOYLE, W. & ROSS, C., 1975, Infant Babbling and Speech, *Journal of Child Language,* 3, 1–11.

PEAL, E. & LAMBERT, W.E., 1962, The Relation of Bilingualism to Intelligence, *Psychological Monographs*, 76, 1–23 (No. 546).

PETERS, A.M., 1977, Language Learning Strategies: Does the Whole Equal the Sum of the Parts?, *Language*, 53, 560–73.

RAMJOUE, B., 1980, *Guidelines for Children's Bilingualism*. Association of American Wives of Europeans, Paris, France.

RONJAT, J., 1913, *Le développement du langage observé chez un enfant bilingue*. Paris: Champion.

SAUNDERS, G., 1982, *Bilingual Children: Guidance for the Family*. Clevedon, England: Multilingual Matters Ltd.

SMITH, N.V., 1973, *The Acquisition of Phonology: A Case Study*. Cambridge: Cambridge University Press.

SNOW, C.E. & FERGUSON, C.A., 1977, *Talking to Children: Language Input & Acquisition*. Cambridge: Cambridge University Press.

STARK, R.E., 1980, Stages of speech development in the first year of life. In G.H. YENI-KOMSHIAN, J.F. KAVANAGH & C.A. FERGUSON (eds), *Child Phonology, Volume 1: Production*. New York: Academic Press.

SVENSSON, G., 1977, *Små invandrarbarn på daghem*. Familjestödsutredningen vid socialdepartementet.

SÖDERBERGH, R., 1979, *Barnets tidiga språkutveckling*. LiberLäromedel Lund.

TAYLOR, M.M., 1974, Speculations on Bilingualism and the Cognitive Network, *Working Papers on Bilingualism*, 2, 68–124.

VIHMAN, M.M., FERGUSON, C.A. & ELBERT, M., in press, Phonological Development from Babbling to Speech: Common Tendencies and Individual Differences, to appear in *Applied Psycholinguistics*.

VOLTERRA, V. & TAESCHNER, T. 1978, The Acquisition and Development of Language by Bilingual Children, *Journal of Child Language*, 5, 311–26.

VYGOTSKY, L., 1974, *Thought and Language*. Cambridge, Mass.: MIT Press.

WELLS, G., 1981, *Learning through Interaction*. Cambridge: Cambridge University Press.

WHITEHURST, G.J., KEDESDY, J. & WHITE, T.G., 1982, A functional analysis of meaning. In S.A. KUCSAJ II (ed.), *Language Development, Vol. 1: Syntax and Semantics*. Hillsdale, N.J.: Lawrence Erlbaum Associates.

Suggestions for further reading

Books/Magazines about Bilingualism and Second Language Learning

ARNBERG, L., 1981, *Early Childhood Bilingualism in the Mixed-Lingual Family.* Doctoral Dissertation, Linköping University, Dept. of Education, S-581 83 Linköping, Sweden. (University Microfilms International No. 82-70,003).

GROSJEAN, F., 1982, *Life with Two Languages: An Introduction to Bilingualism.* Cambridge, Mass.: Harvard University Press.

MCLAUGHLIN, B., 1984, *Second-Language Acquisition in Childhood: Vol. 1. Preschool Children* (Second Edition). Hillsdale, N.J.: Lawrence Erlbaum Associates.

— 1985, *Second-Language Acquisition in Childhood: Vol. 2. School-Age Children* (Second Edition). Hillsdale, N.J.: Lawrence Erlbaum Associates.

SAUNDERS, G., 1982, *Bilingual Children: Guidance for the Family.* Clevedon, England: Multilingual Matters Ltd.

VENTRILIGA, L., 1982, *Conversations of Miguel and Maria: How Children Learn English as a Second Language.* Reading, Mass.: Addison-Wesley.

The Bilingual Family Newsletter. Published by Multilingual Matters Ltd. Address:

Bank House, 8a Hill Road
Clevedon, Avon
England BS21 7HH

Books about Language Development in General

HOLZMAN, M., 1983, *The Language of Children: Development in Home and School.* Englewood Cliffs, N.J.: Prentice-Hall, Inc.

MACAULAY, R., 1980, *Generally Speaking: How Children Learn Language.* Rowley, Mass.: Newbury House.

Books about Stimulating Young Children's Learning (Including Language Development As Well As Other Areas)

ANDERSSON, T., 1981, *A Guide to Family Reading in Two Languages: The Preschool Years.* Los Angeles, Ca.: Evaluation, Dissemination and Assessment Center, California State University.

DOMAN, G., 1975, *How to Teach Your Baby to Read.* Garden City, N.Y.: Doubleday & Company, Inc.

HONIG, A.C., 1982, *Playtime Learning Games for Young Children.* Syracuse, N.Y.: Syracuse University Press.

GORDON, I.J., GUINAGH, B. & JESTER, R.E., 1972, *Child Learning Through Child Play: Learning Activities for Two and Three Year Olds.* New York: St. Martin's Press.

STEIN, S.B., 1976, *New Parents Guide to Early Learning.* New York: New American Library.

Books about Starting Play-groups and about Childcare Programmes for Young Children in General

BROAD, L.P. & BUTTERWORTH, N.T., 1974, *The Playgroup Handbook.* New York: St. Martin's Press.

CATALDO, C.Z., 1983, *Infant & Toddler Programs: A Guide to Very Early Childhood Education.* Reading, Mass.: Addison-Wesley.

LUCAS, J. & HENDERSON, A., 1981, *Pre-School Playgroups: A Handbook.* London: George Allen & Unwin.

WINN, M. & PORCHER, M.A., 1967, *The Playgroup Book.* Fontana/Collins.

Index